Sonia Boyce

Lygia Clark

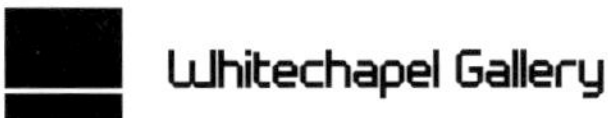
Whitechapel Gallery

Published on the occasion
of the exhibitions
Lygia Clark: The I and the You
Sonia Boyce: An Awkward Relation
Whitechapel Gallery, London: 2 October
2024 -12 January 2025

EXHIBITIONS

WHITECHAPEL GALLERY
Director: Gilane Tawadros
Curators: Michael Asbury, Sonia Boyce,
Gilane Tawadros
Interim Head of Exhibitions: Sophie Clark
Former Head of Exhibitions: Elena Crippa
Curator, Special Projects: Katrina Schwarz
Assistant Curator: Hannah Woods
Curatorial Assistant: Carolina Jozami
Gallery Technical Manager: Luke Edwards

WHITECHAPEL GALLERY STAFF
Syara Ahmed, Shohid Ahmed, Gözde
Altun, Sadika Begum, Fatima Begum,
Edgar Bird, Olivia Blyth, Sue Bowley,
Daniel John Bracken, Christy Chan, Ellie
Clowes, Claudia Contu, Joel Cosson,
Camilla Cuminatti, Harry Curtoys,
Pedro da Costa, Anh Tuan Dao, Helen
Davison, Asa Desouza-Jones, Alan
Diamond, Aggie Dolan, Luke Edwards,
Molly Evans, Gabriella Fabbriani, Misha
Farrant, Shirin Fathi, Will Ferreira Dyke,
Cameron Foote, Freya Gascoyne,
Alejandra Gissler, Olivia Gomes, Luke
Gregory-Jones, Ali Hafiz, Leila Hasham,
Majharul Islam, Yulia Ivanova, Carolina
Laia Jozami, Jacqueline Kent, Hana Khan,
Andrey Lazarev, Eden Leeds, Kirsty
Lowry Smith, Ewa Luc, Aili Markelius,
Richard Martin, Colette McNulty, Katerina
Mesterovic, Luis Mondejar, Nezliya
Muhara, Gemma Murray, Rummana
Naqvi, Jade Nicklin, Amelia Oakley,
Pianka Pärna, Elsie Plimmer, Natasha
Plowright, Katherine Proudlove, Alice-
Anne Psaltis, Agostino Quaranta, Raffia
Rahman, Mabrur Rahman, Martin Reyes,
Ella Ross-Leahy, Rishika Sahgal, Katrina
Schwarz, Francesca Scott-Sills, Vicky
Steer, Allan Struthers, Tamanna Sultana,
Sean Synnuck, Gilane Tawadros, Alice
Thompson Taika Tontti, Katie Town, Lucie
Treinen, Muhammad Uddin, Tamara
Ustenko, Drupesh Vekaria, Thomas
Watson, Sam Williams, Yuk Wun Jade
Wong, Florence Wong, Oscar Woodiwiss,
Hannah Woods, Andrea Ziemer-Masefield

PUBLICATION

Publications Coordinator: Joel Cosson
Copy Editor: Linda Schofield

Designed by Giulia Garbin
Assisted by Juliet Ramsden
Printed by Gomer, Wales

ISBN: 978-0-85488-324-0

First published 2024
by Whitechapel Gallery

Whitechapel Gallery

Whitechapel Gallery
77–82 Whitechapel High Street London,
E1 7QX whitechapelgallery.org

Distributed outside the United States
and Canada by Thames & Hudson
181a High Holborn London,
WC1V 7QX Tel: +44 (0)20 7845 5000
sales@thameshudson.co.uk

Distributed in the United States
and Canada by Artbook / D.A.P.
75 Broad Street, Suite 630 New York, NY
10004 Tel: +1 (212) 627 199

Lygia Clark: The I and the You and *Sonia Boyce: An Awkward Relation* have been generously supported by:
Cockayne – Grants for the Arts: a donor advised fund held at The London Community Foundation
Hauser & Wirth
Henry Moore Foundation
The TrAIN Research Centre at University of the Arts London
The Lygia Clark and Sonia Boyce Exhibition Circles

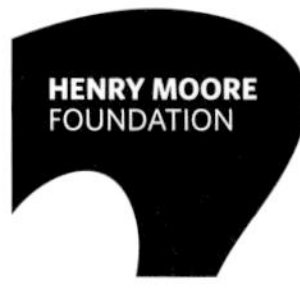

With additional thanks to:
Alison Jacques, London
APALAZZOGALLERY
Associacao Cultural Lygia Clark
Embassy of Brazil in London/ Instituto Guimarães Rosa
LATAM Airlines
OMNI colour

Whitechapel Gallery would like to thank:

MAJOR DONORS AND SUPPORTERS
Arts Council England Catalyst Endowment Fund
Sir Frank Bowling
Bloomberg Philanthropies
D. Daskalopoulos Collection
Ford Foundation
Foyle Foundation
Freelands Foundation
Collezione Maramotti
Max Mara
Paul Mellon Centre for Studies in British Art
The Rose Foundation
Terra Foundation for American Art
Michael & Nina Zilkha
and those that wish to remain anonymous

EXHIBITIONS PROGRAMME
A/POLITICAL
Aldgate Connect BID
Erin Bell
Cockayne – Grants for the Arts
Collezione Maramotti
Fluxus Art Projects
Selma Feriani Gallery
Goodman Gallery
Hauser & Wirth
Hiscox
Institut français of Paris
Max Mara
Mennour, Paris
Paul Mellon Centre for Studies in British Art
Richard Saltoun Gallery
Maria and Malek Sukkar
Michael Zilkha
The Whitechapel Gallery Commissioning Council
The Whitechapel Gallery Patrons
and those who wish to remain anonymous

EDUCATION & PUBLIC PROGRAMMES
The 29th May 1961 Charitable Trust
Aldgate Connect BID
Capital Group
Kurt Forrest Foundation
Phillips
Tower Hamlets Arts & Music Education Service (THAMES)
The London Borough of Tower Hamlets
Stanley Picker Trust
The Whitechapel Gallery Education Council

WHITECHAPEL GALLERY CORPORATE PATRONS AND MEMBERS
Alma
Bloomberg Philanthropies
Frasers Property UK
Gazelli Art House
Lisson Gallery
Phillips

WHITECHAPEL GALLERY CORPORATE SUPPORTERS
Aldgate Connect BID
Bloomberg Philanthropies
Champagne Pommery
Crozier Fine Arts
Fredrigoni
Hiscox (Artworks Insurance Partner)
Max Mara
Collezione Maramotti
Omni Colour (Signage Partner)
Phillips

WHITECHAPEL GALLERY COMMISSIONING COUNCIL
Dorota Audemars
Erin Bell
Émilie De Pauw
Irene Panagopoulos
Nicole Saikalis Bay

WHITECHAPEL GALLERY EDUCATION COUNCIL
Julie and Debashis Dey
Alex Sainsbury

WHITECHAPEL GALLERY GLOBAL CIRCLE
Yan Du
Faisal Tamer and Sara Alireza
and those who wish to remain anonymous

WHITECHAPEL GALLERY DIRECTOR'S CIRCLE
Erin Bell & Michael Cohen
Pilar Corrias
Julie & Debashis Dey
Rami Kim
Bimpe Nkontchou
Anthea Peers
Thatcher & Jill Thompson
and those who wish to remain anonymous

WHITECHAPEL GALLERY CURATOR'S CIRCLE
Annette Anthony
Adrian & Jennifer O'Carroll
Oba Nsugbe
Audrey Wallrock
and those who wish to remain anonymous

WHITECHAPEL GALLERY PATRONS
Malgosia Alterman
Cedric Bardawil
Sadie Coles HQ
Francesca Consigli
Sarah Elson
Joanna & Alan Gemes
Mark Harris
Pippy Houldsworth
Marie Krauss
Frank Krikhaar
Kate MacGarry
Mary E McNicholas
Heike Moras
Maureen Paley
Dominic Palfreyman
Darryl de Prez & Victoria Thomas
Maria-Cruz Rashidian
Marina Roncarolo
Marina Ruiz-Colomer
Alex Sainsbury & Elinor Jansz
Cherrill & Ian Scheer
Veronica Schwabach
Elisabeth von Schwarzkopf
Amar Singh
Karen & Mark Smith
Bina & Philippe von Stauffenberg
Christoph & Marion Trestler
and those who wish to remain anonymous

We remain grateful for the ongoing support of Whitechapel Gallery Members.

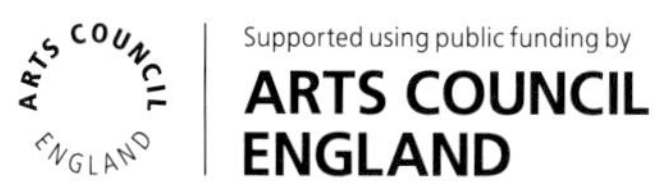

Whitechapel Gallery is proud to be a National Portfolio Organisation of Arts Council England.

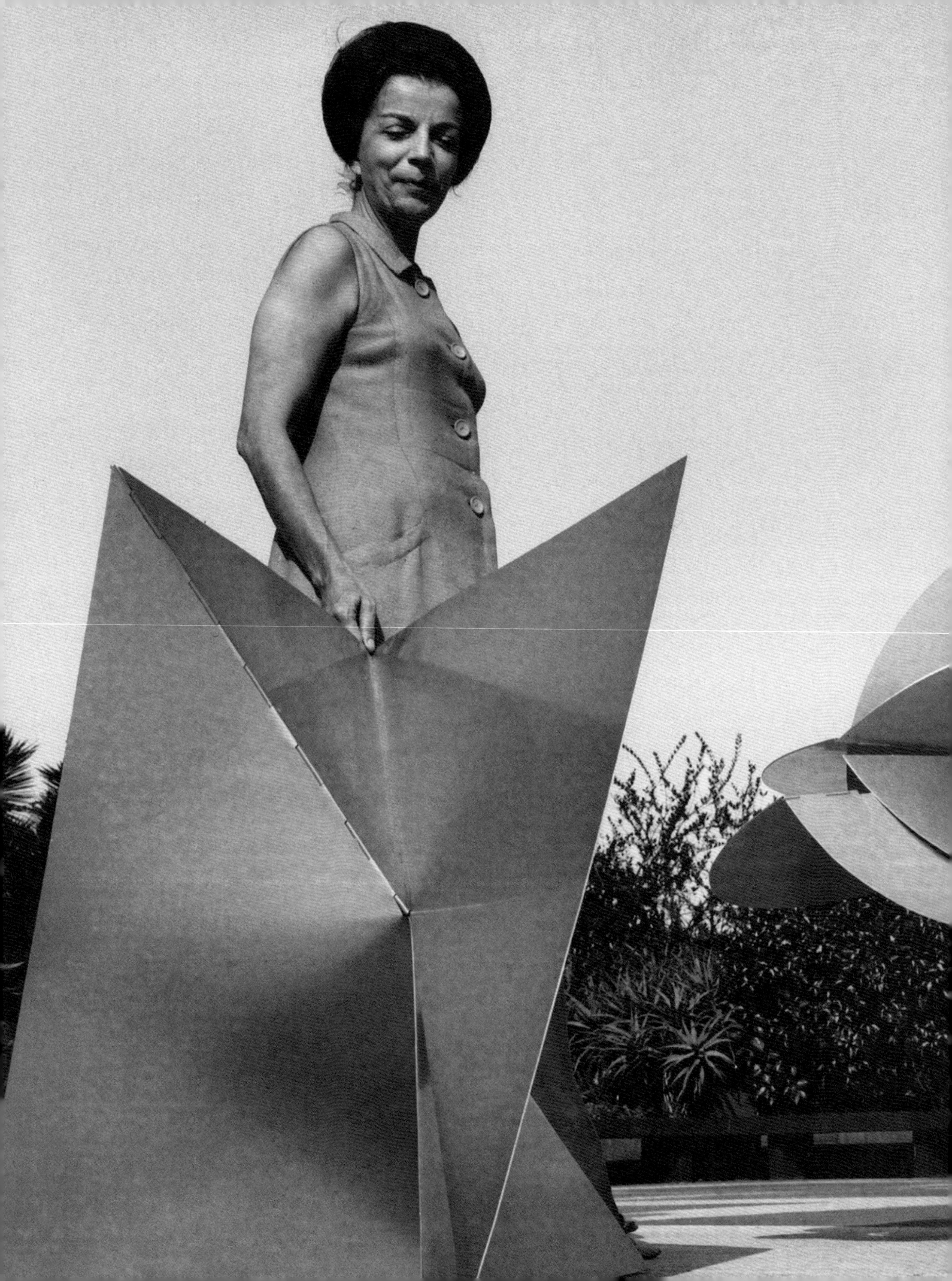

← Lygia Clark and *Bicho Ponta*
courtesy Associação Cultural O Mundo de Lygia Clark

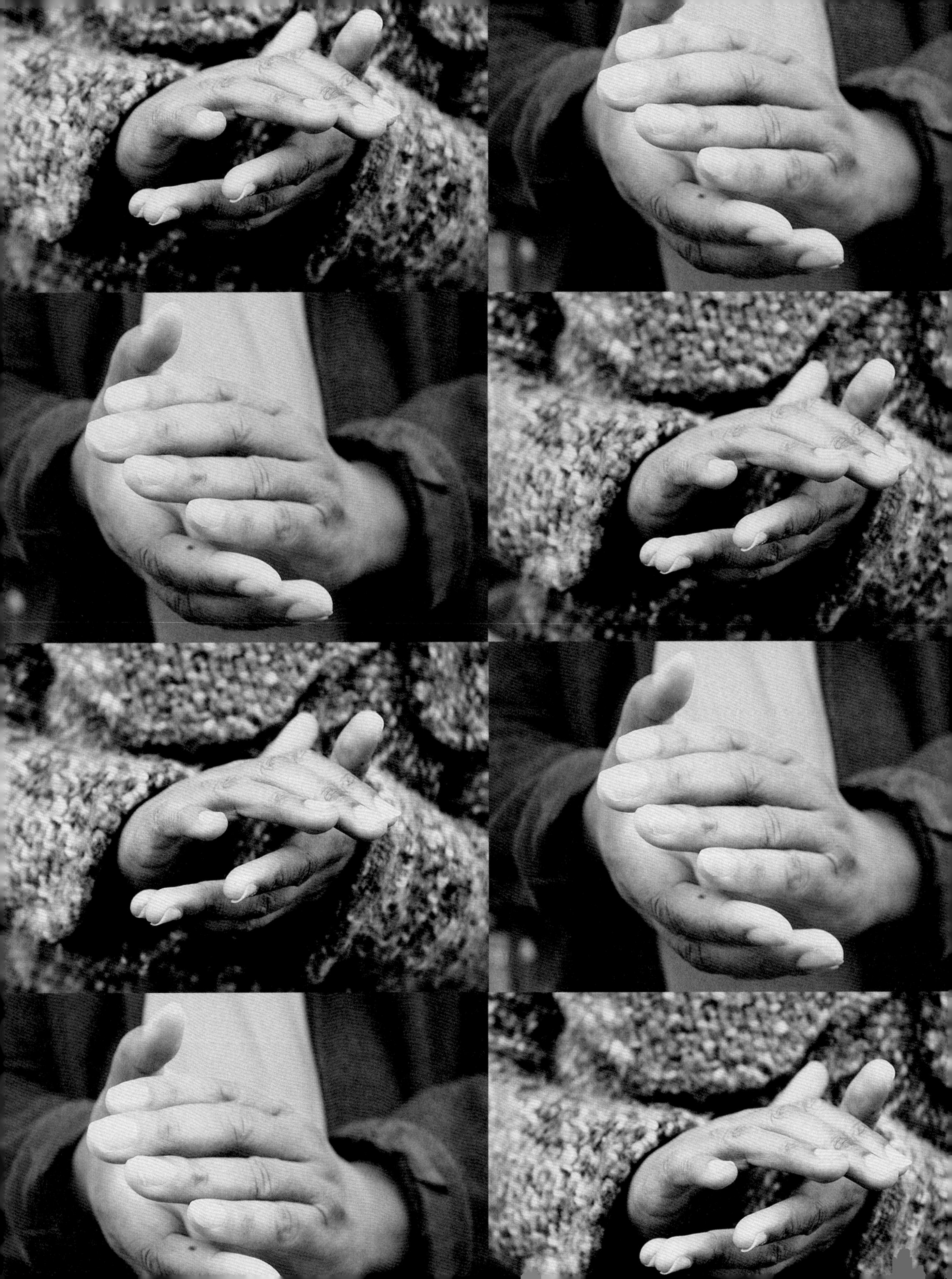

Foreword

In the very first issue of the art journal *Third Text* (autumn 1987), edited by the artist Rasheed Araeen, an interview between the art critic John Roberts and the British artist Sonia Boyce preceded an essay by the art critic and curator Guy Brett on the Brazilian artist Lygia Clark, entitled 'Lygia Clark: the borderline between art and life'. More than three decades later, Whitechapel Gallery has brought Lygia Clark and Sonia Boyce together again with two exhibitions presented in dialogue with each other: 'Lygia Clark: The I and the You' (named after a work by Clark from 1967 that is now in the collection of the Museum of Modern Art in New York) and 'Sonia Boyce: An Awkward Relation'. The exhibitions explore pivotal moments in the artists' careers, when each began experimenting with participatory practices.

Both artists have had a long relationship with Whitechapel Gallery. The Gallery hosted a Sonia Boyce exhibition in 1988, which followed on from her inclusion in the group exhibition 'From Two Worlds' in 1986 and her participation in the pioneering Artists in East London Schools Scheme in 1985. Over the years, Whitechapel Gallery has played a significant role in championing art from Latin America, including presenting exhibitions of the work of Hélio Oiticica, Frida Kahlo, Tina Modotti, Tunga and Alfredo Jaar. Lygia Clark's works have featured previously in two group exhibitions at the Gallery: Catherine De Zegher's historic exhibition 'Inside the Visible' (1996) and the group exhibition 'Three Towards Infinity: New Multiple Art' (1970).

'The I and the You' marks the first major UK public gallery survey of the pioneering and influential artist Lygia Clark, and is co-curated by Anglo-Brazilian scholar Michael Asbury, Sonia Boyce and myself. The exhibition focuses on Clark's artistic journey from the mid 1950s to the early 1970s, a particularly volatile period in Brazil's history when radical modes of artistic practice also emerged. Clark was a central figure in the Brazilian Neoconcrete movement (1959–61) alongside

← Sonia Boyce, *Clapping Wallpaper*, 1994 (reprinted 2009)
digital repeat pattern on wallpaper, dimensions variable

fellow artists such as Amílcar de Castro, Ferreira Gullar, Hélio Oiticica and Lygia Pape (among others), who were frustrated by what they felt were the limitations of Concrete art and its emphasis on non-figurative geometric abstraction. Instead, Neoconcrete artists began to push for greater experimentation, expression, colour and poetic sensibility in their practices, as well as proposing a shift in how audiences might participate in artworks.

'The I and the You' reveals how Clark's early formal experimentation and growing interest in the philosophy of experience and therapeutic potential of art led her to find new ways for audiences to physically interact with her artworks, furthering her interest in the relationship between object and viewer, internal and external, self and world. Over the course of the 1960s, Clark's work increasingly prioritised embodied experience over the symbolic status of the object. Her materials included plastic bags, paper, glue, stones, elastic bands and fruit netting, which she repurposed, inviting and encouraging a range of experiences and propositions.

Sonia Boyce's 'An Awkward Relation' brings together a number of pivotal and rarely seen works to explore themes of interaction, participation and improvisation, all of which have played a definitive role in Boyce's practice since the 1990s and reflect a shared interest with many of the radical approaches that Lygia Clark pioneered in her work.

Boyce was introduced to Clark's work in the 1990s and felt a strong synergy with the Brazilian artist's experiential and participatory practice. 'An Awkward Relation' explores the feelings of both involvement and uneasiness intrinsic to an approach that invites visitors to engage, touch and experience artworks and their surroundings in new and unscripted ways. The title of the exhibition is indicative of this complex, often difficult, relationship between artists, works and audiences. It also recognises that while there are similarities between Boyce's and Clark's work, there are also clear differences that necessarily, and inevitably, stem from the very different artistic, geographical and sociopolitical contexts in which the artists were working.

'An Awkward Relation' features some of Boyce's hair 'sculptures' made from human and synthetic hair, which were originally included in the 'Do You Want to Touch?' exhibition at 181 Gallery, London, in 1993. The works address and confront deep-seated desires and assumptions, with visitors invited to touch and respond to the display instinctively and directly. These themes are also explored in the 50 collages *Black Female Hairstyles* (1995) and the video work *Exquisite Tension* (2006), as well as a number of photographic works that document and consider hair through the lens of race and gender. The exhibition culminates with the seven-channel multimedia installation *We move in her way* (2017), developed from the documentation of Boyce's performance of the same name that took place at the Institute of Contemporary Arts, London, in 2016. Partly inspired by Clark's work from the late 1960s to the early 1970s, there are also references to the Dadaist Sophie Taeuber-Arp. The original performance of *We move in her way* unfolds organically, with performers asked to improvise and interact with the audience in attendance. The installation at Whitechapel Gallery is framed within bespoke geometric structures and kaleidoscopic wallpapers, key elements of Boyce's recent practice.

Although separated by time and geography, and working in different cultural and sociopolitical contexts, Lygia Clark and Sonia Boyce share a deep interest in addressing and shifting the relationship between artist, artwork and audiences, often inviting visitors to touch or manipulate, or even inhabit, their works. By pairing the two artists in this way, we are inviting audiences to reflect on both the similarities and differences in their works and approaches, while also providing a meeting point for different art histories and cultural contexts. It feels particularly timely to present the work of these artists together at this moment when their shared interest in participatory practice and experimentation with form resonates with a younger generation of artists, curators and audiences concerned with questions of care and participation in contemporary art.

We are deeply indebted to Sonia Boyce, Michael Asbury and the Associação Cultural Lygia Clark without whom the exhibition 'Lygia Clark: The I and the You' would not have been possible. Our special thanks go to the President of the Association Eduardo Clark and its Secretary General Juliano Werneck. We would also like to thank Michael Wellen at Tate Modern and Alison Jacques and Martin Coppell at Alison Jacques, London for their advice and support, and Guilherme Torres and Paul Jenkins at Almeida & Dale. We are extremely grateful to the Brazilian ambassador His Excellency Antônio Patriota and his team, in particular Ana Flavia Jacintho Bonzanini and Marcio Junji, who have been so supportive of this project from the beginning. We would also like to thank Alex Brown, Dominic Johnson, Paul Heritage and Rosie

10

Hunter from Queen Mary University of London for their advice on the live performance element of this exhibition, and to Cockayne – Grants for the Arts: a donor advised fund held at The London Community Foundation, Henry Moore Foundation and the TrAIN research centre at University of the Arts London for their generous financial support.

Sonia Boyce's exhibition 'An Awkward Relation' would not have been possible without the wonderful support of her studio manager Niamh Sullivan and her project assistant Ruth Hogan. We are indebted to Hauser and Wirth for their generous support, in particular Corinne Bannister, Judith Nezri, Neil Wenman and Iwan and Manuela Wirth, and we are also grateful for the support from Valeria Gemelli and Francesca Migliorati of APALAZZOGALLERY and Cockayne – Grants for the Arts: a donor advised fund held at The London Community Foundation.

We are extremely grateful to all the lenders who have so generously loaned works to these exhibitions. Special thanks are also due to Katrina Schwarz, Hannah Woods, Luke Edwards, Carolina Jozami, Elena Crippa and Sophie Clark for their work on the exhibitions, and to Joel Cosson and Giulia Garbin for their work on this publication.

Gilane Tawadros

Lygia Clark, *Diálogo de Mãos* (Hand dialogue), 1968 →
photograph by Eduardo Clark, courtesy Associação Cultural O Mundo de Lygia Clark

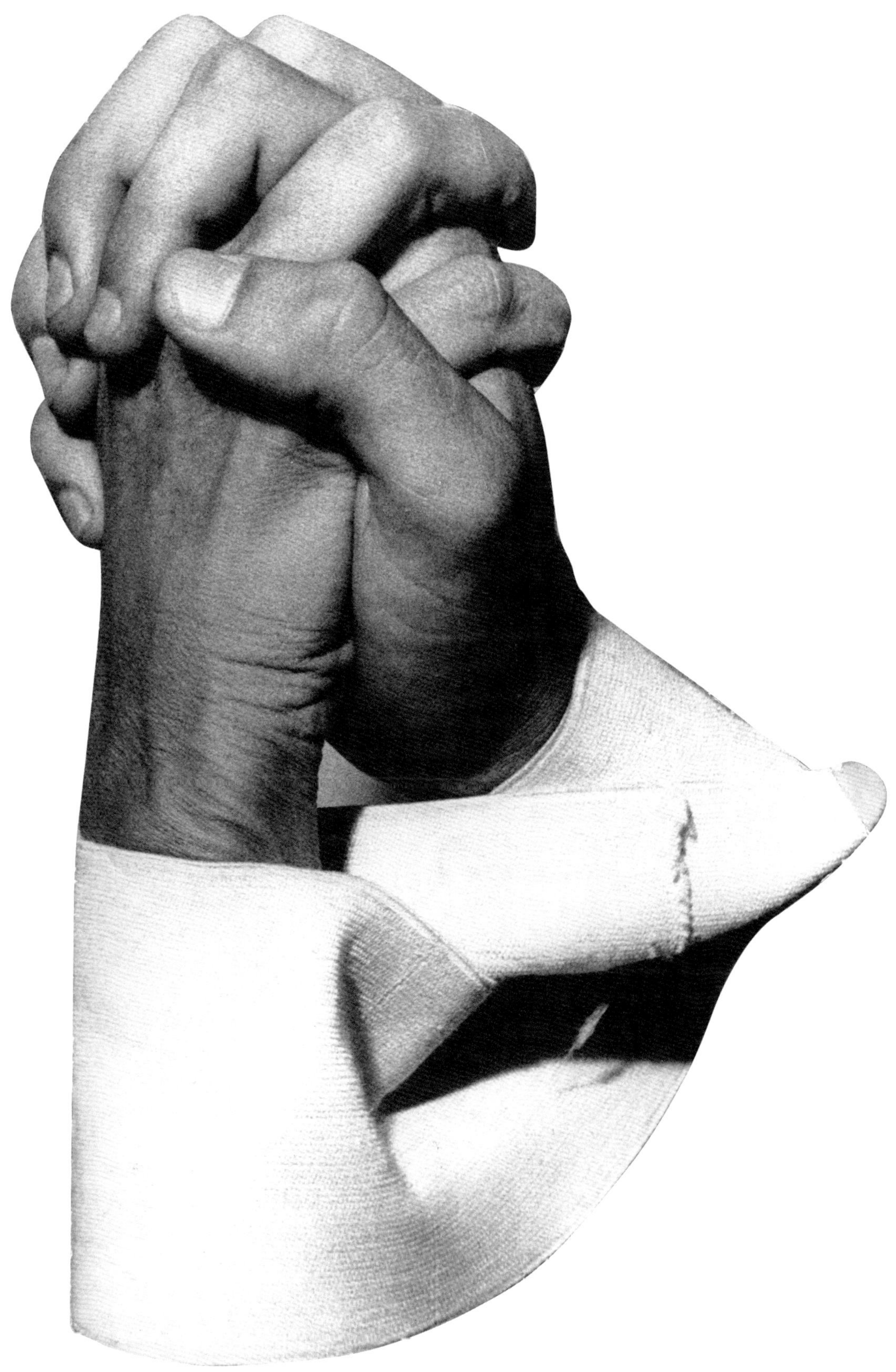

Sonia Boyce

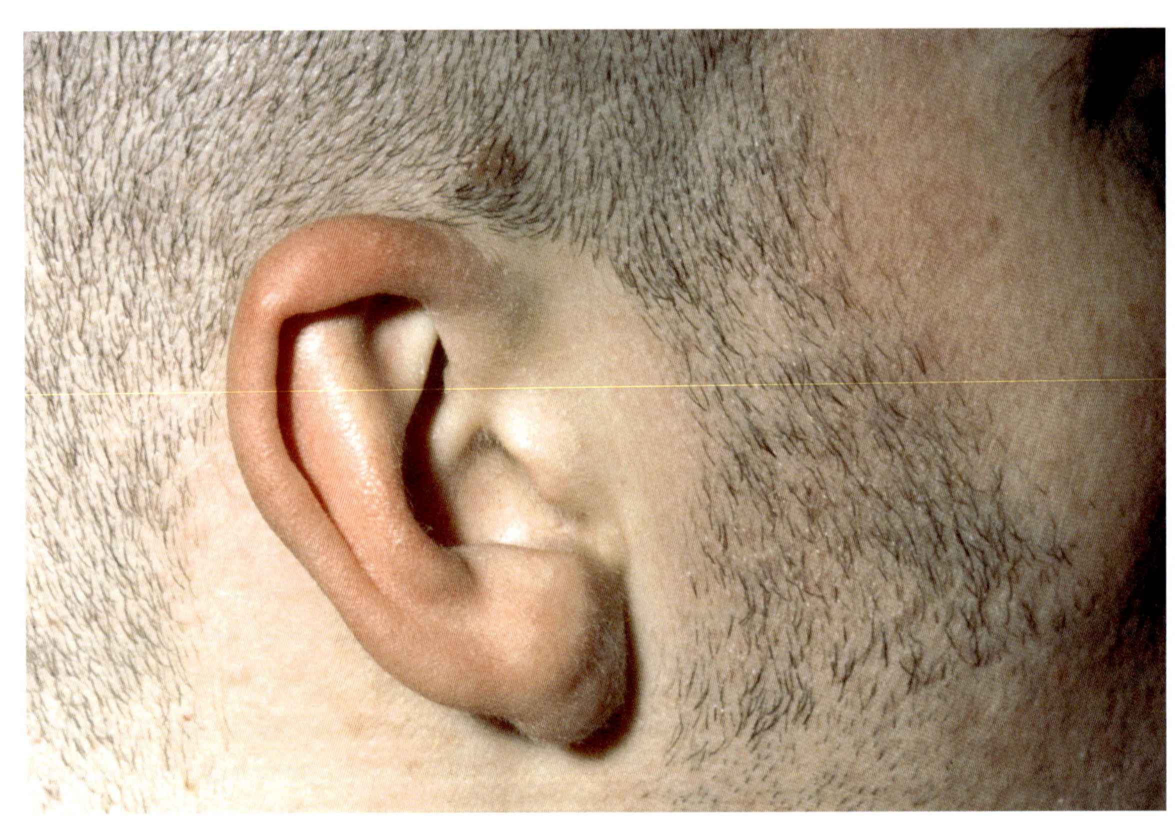

Sonia Boyce, *Head I (Skin)*, 1995
photographic print on dibond, 91.5 x 137.5 cm

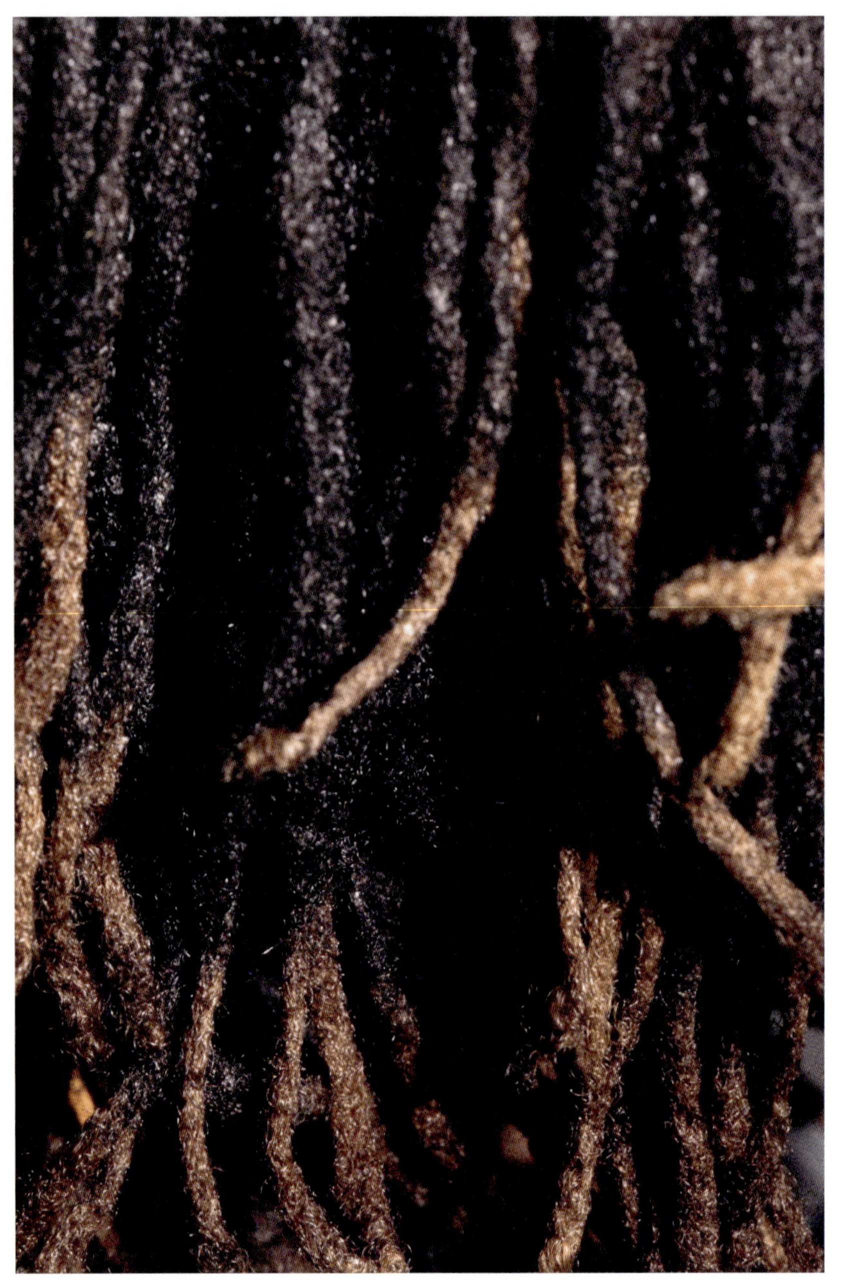

Sonia Boyce, *Head II (Dread)*, 1995
photographic print on dibond, 137.5 x 91.5 cm

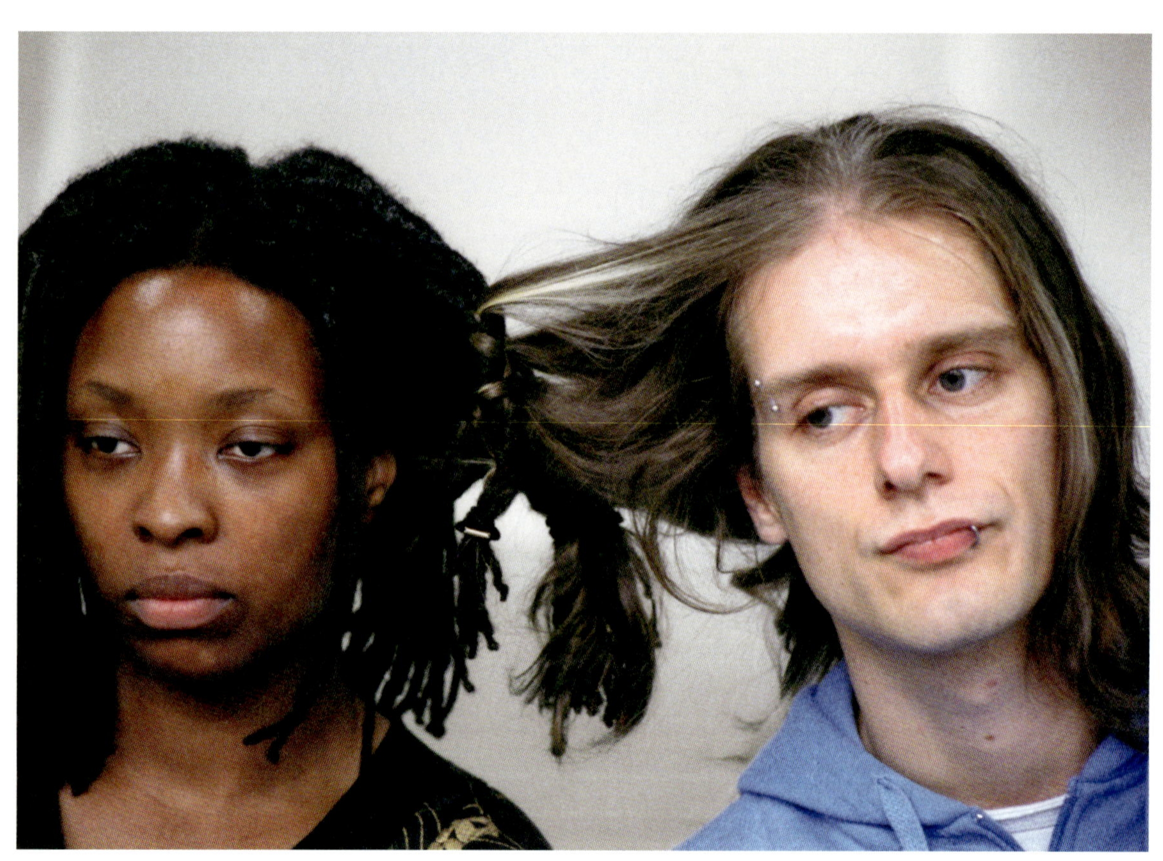

Sonia Boyce, *Exquisite Tension*, 2006
single-channel SD colour video with sound
video duration: 4 minutes

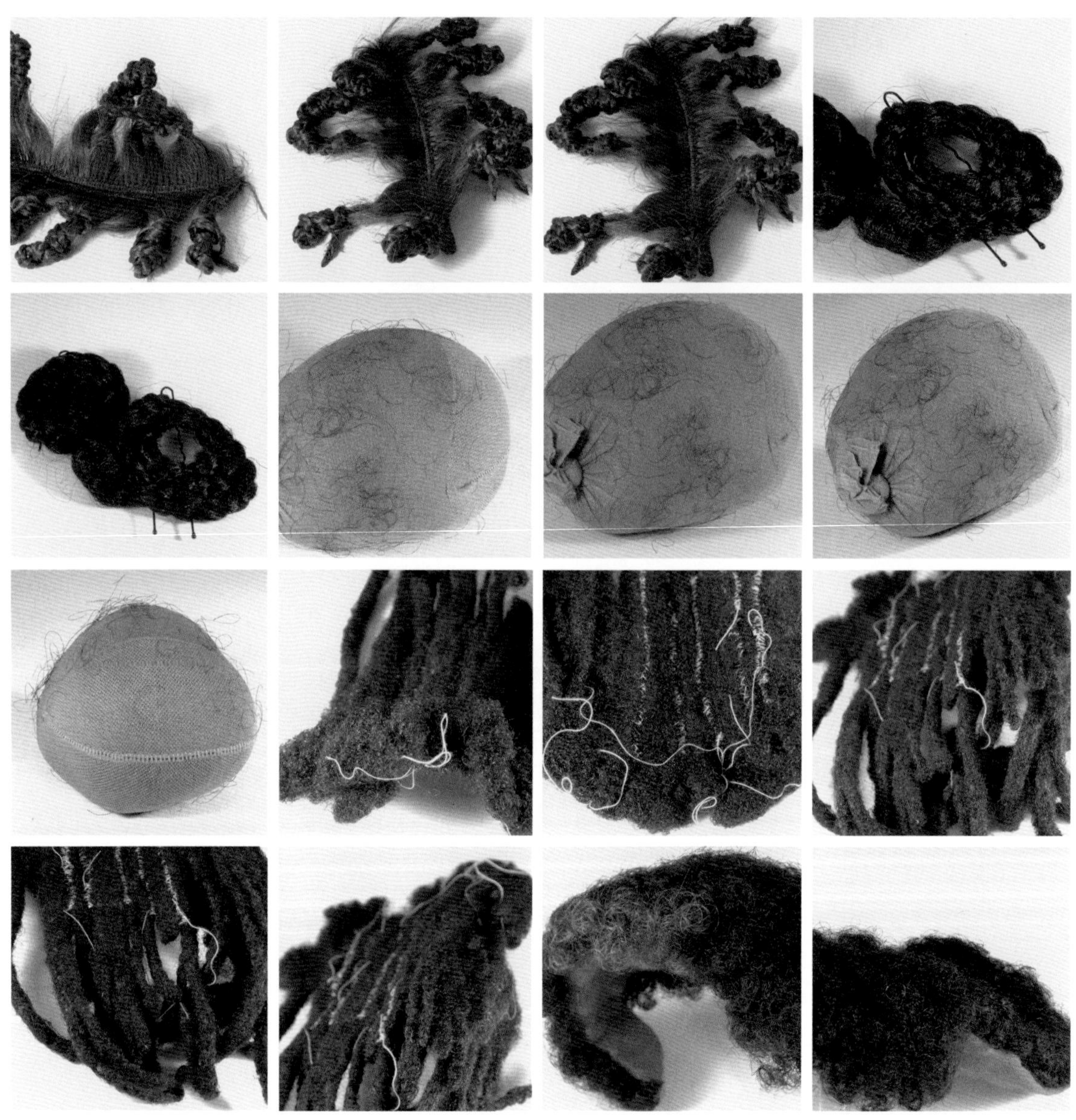

Sonia Boyce, *Hair Objects Grid*, 1994 (printed 2016)
photographic print on dibond, 80 x 80 cm

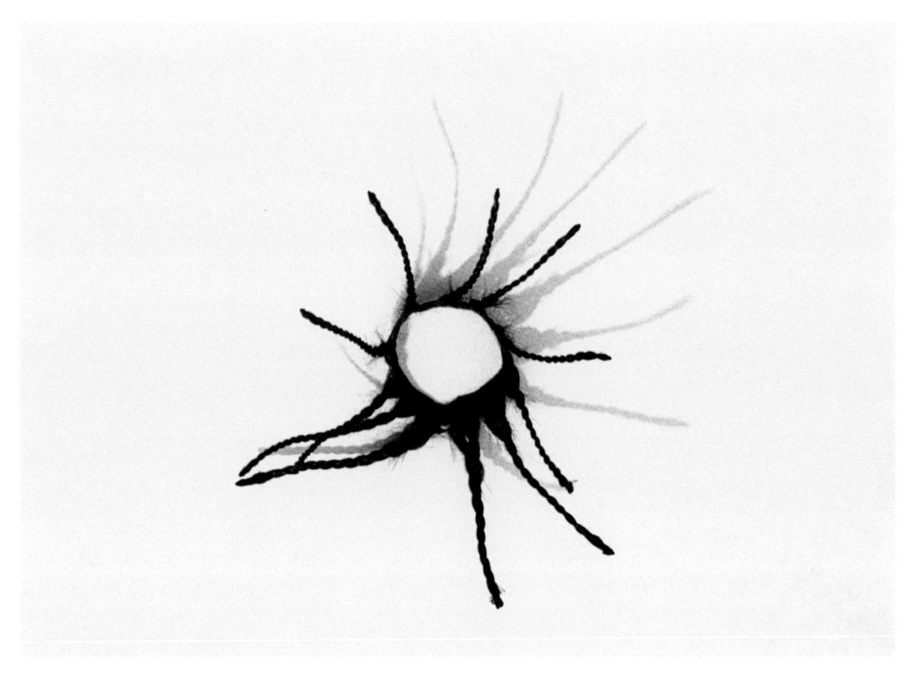

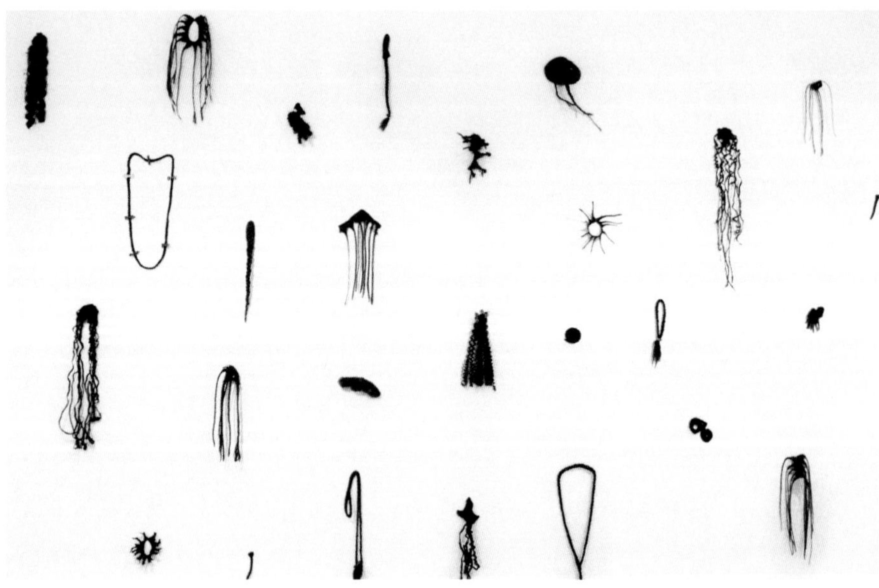

Sonia Boyce, *Do You Want to Touch?*, 1993
installation view and detail, 181 Gallery, Hammersmith, London

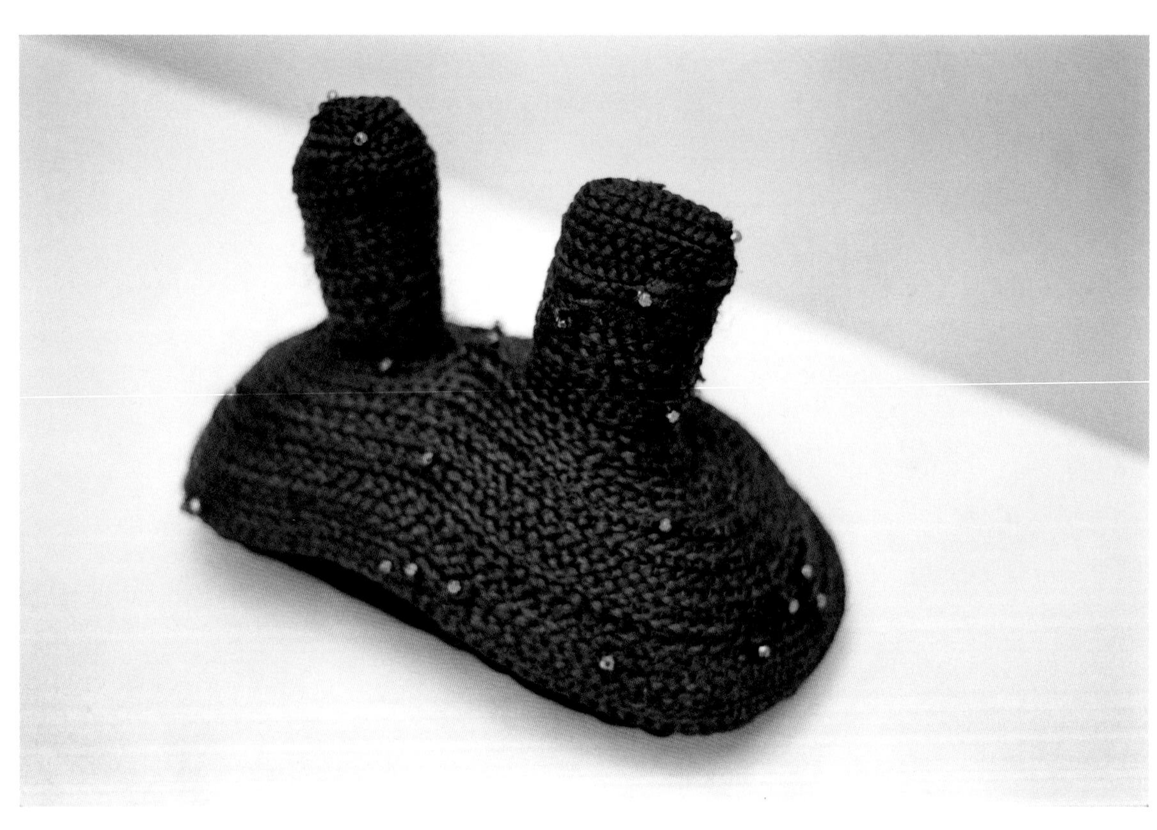

Sonia Boyce, *The Comforter*, 1993
braided hair sewn, beads, velvet, 26 x 17 x 12 cm

25

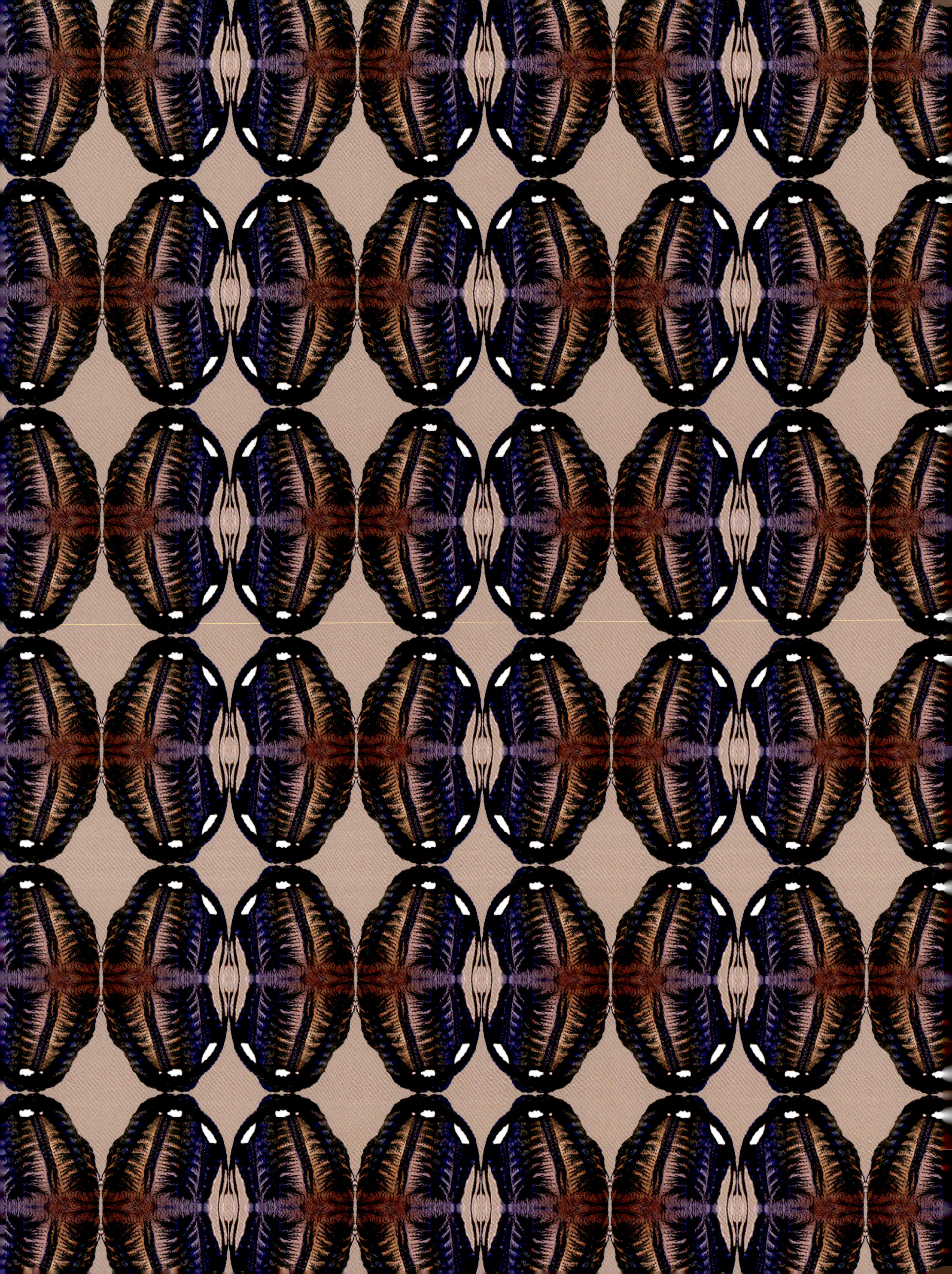

Sonia Boyce, *Braided Wallpaper*, 2023
digital repeat pattern on tan wallpaper, dimensions variable

27

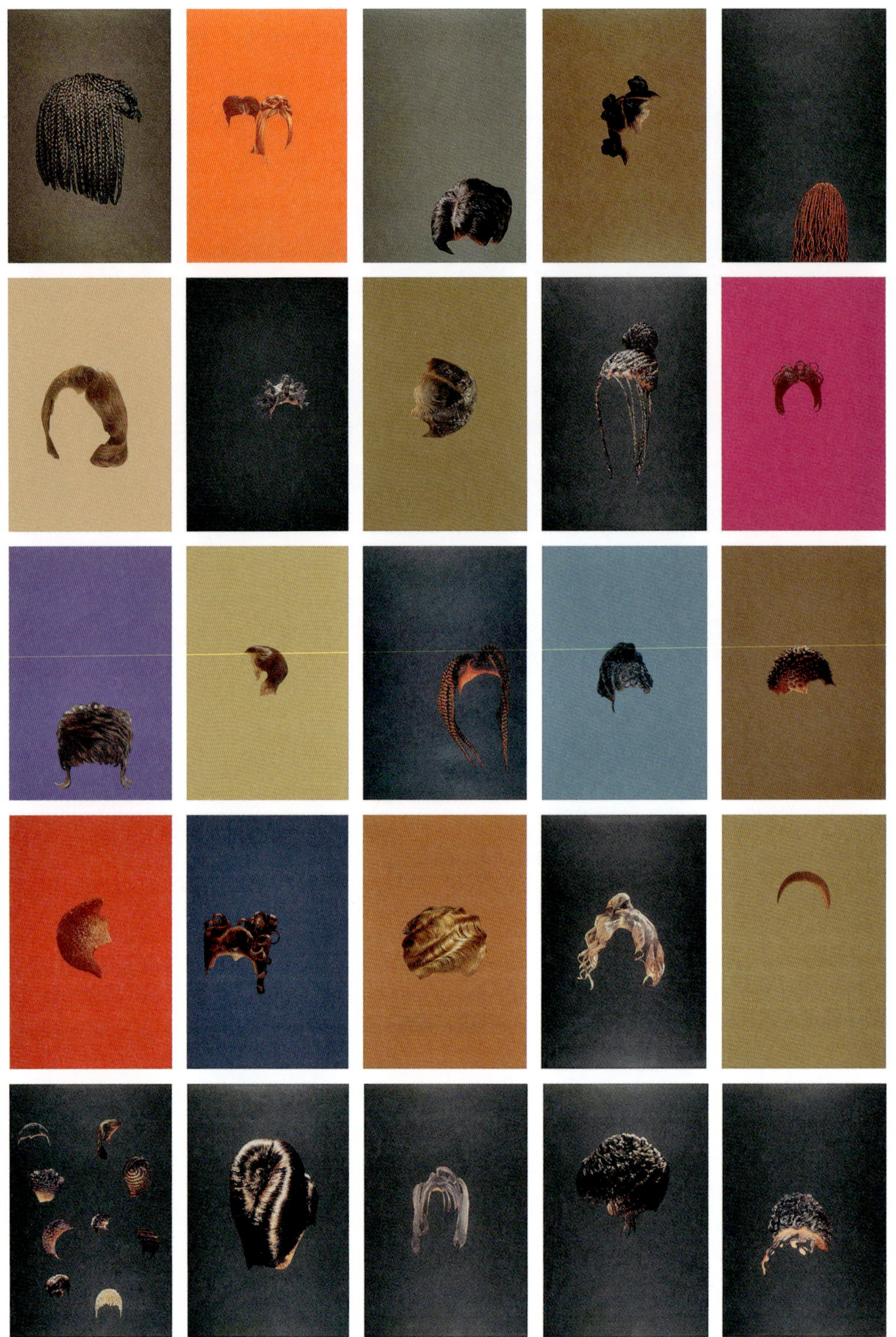

Sonia Boyce, *Black Female Hairstyles*, 1995
collages on paper, 113 x 156 cm

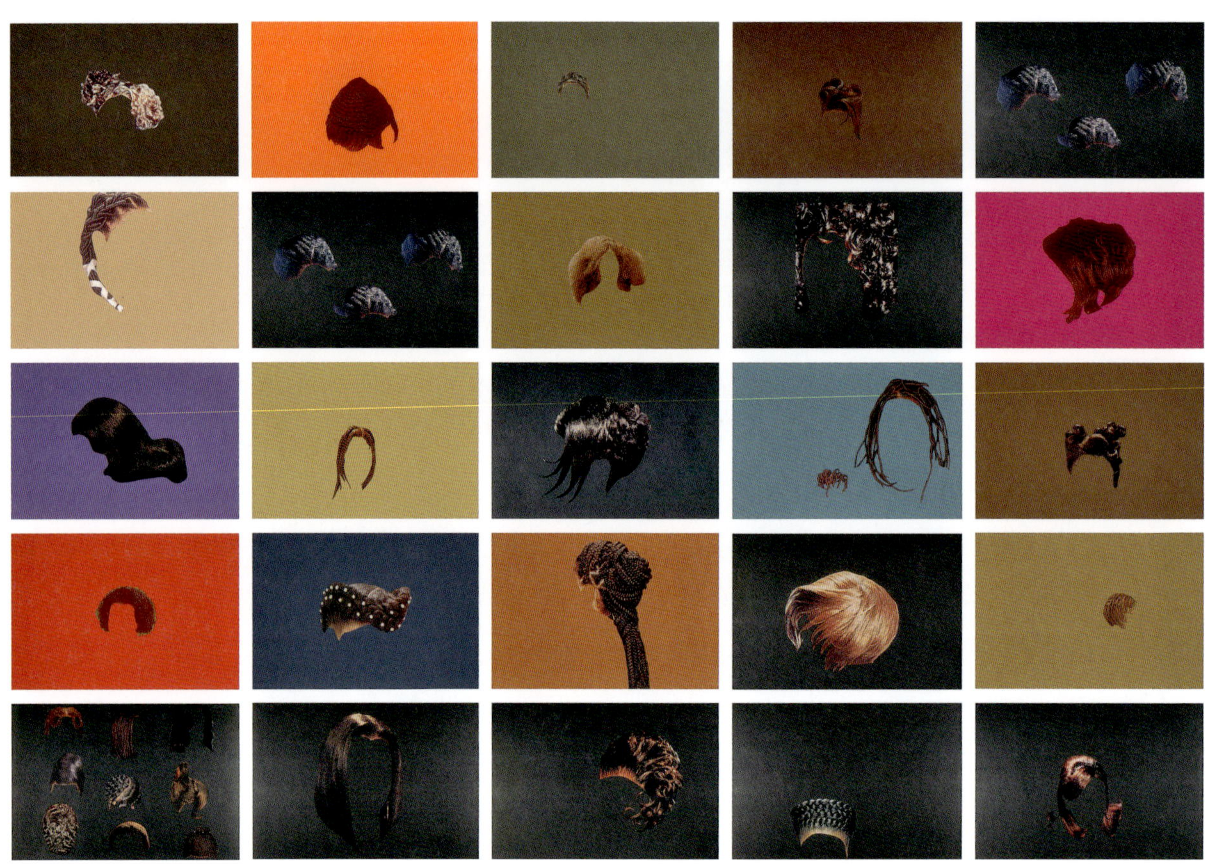

Sonia Boyce, *Black Female Hairstyles*, 1995
collages on paper, 156 x 113 cm

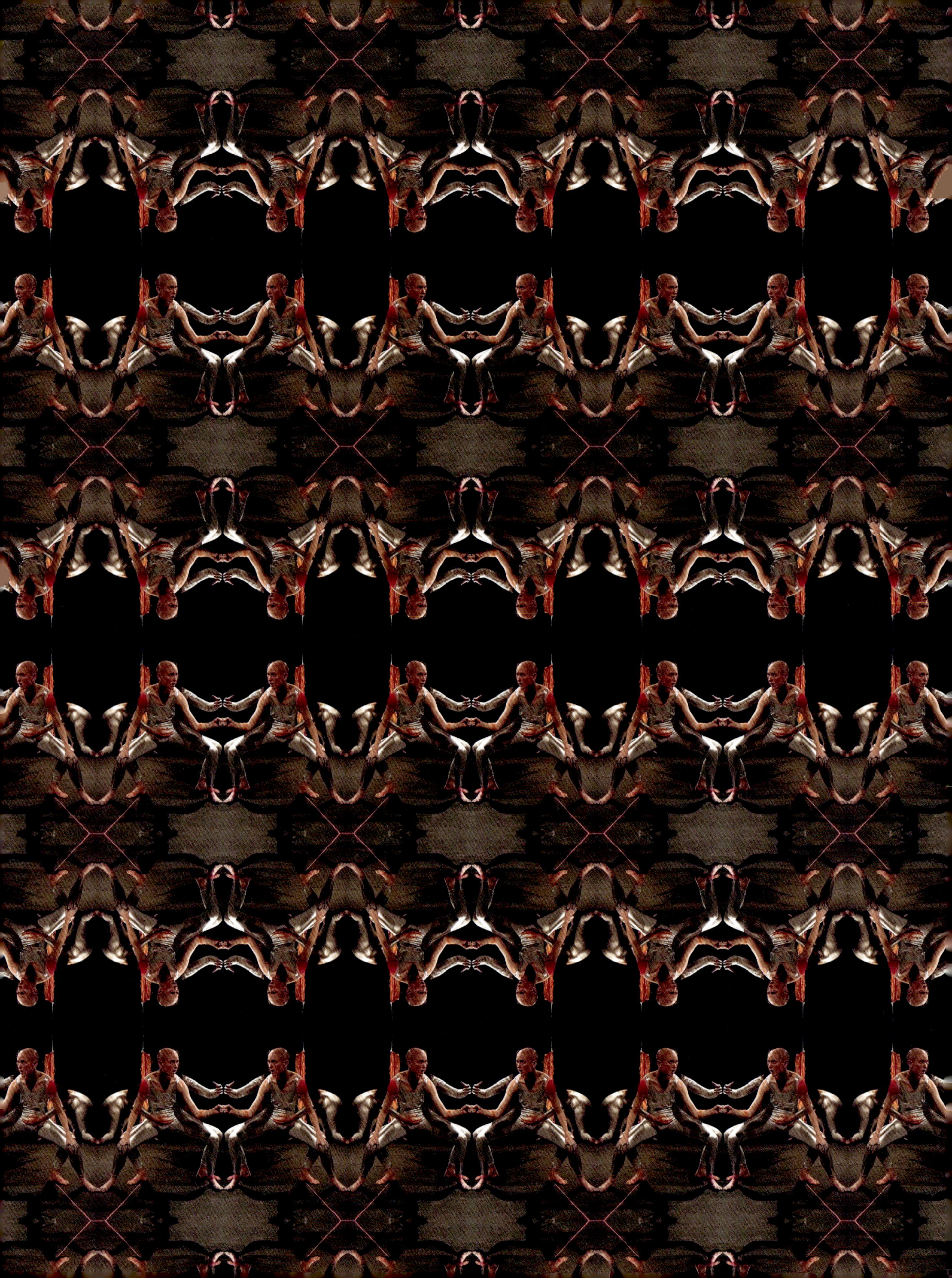

Sonia Boyce, *We move in her way Eve and Be Wallpaper*, 2017
digital repeat pattern on vinyl, dimensions variable

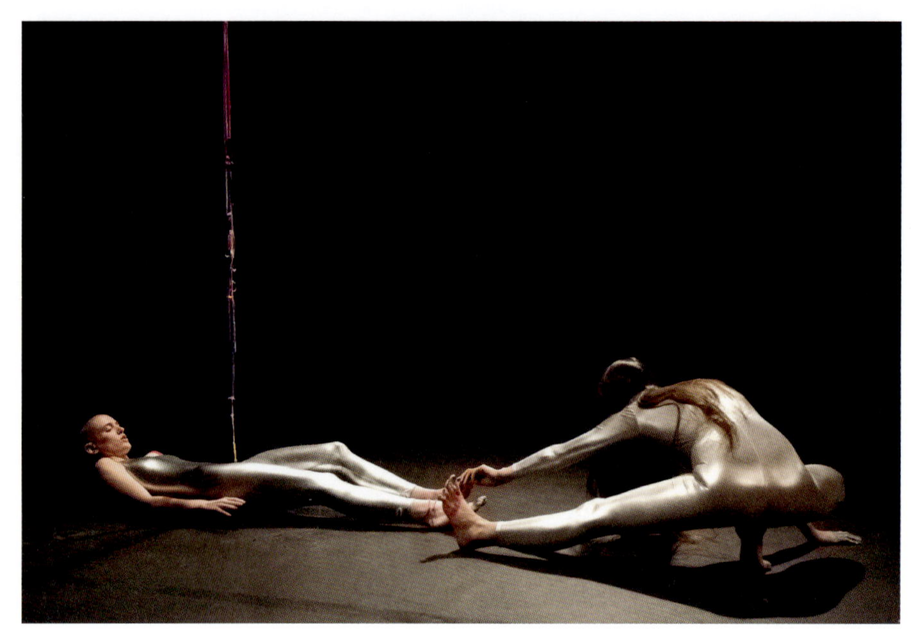

Sonia Boyce, *We move in her way* (production still), 2016
photograph by George Torode

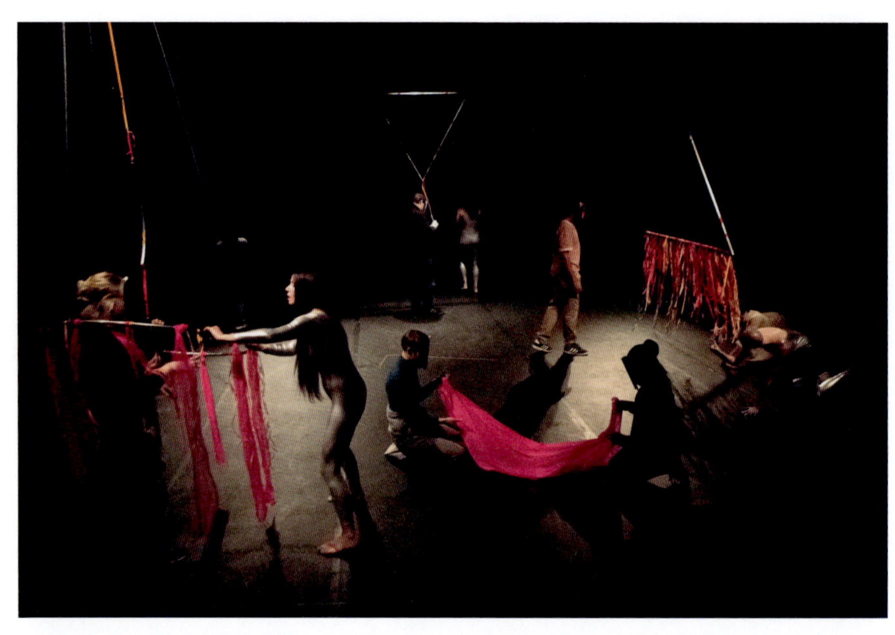

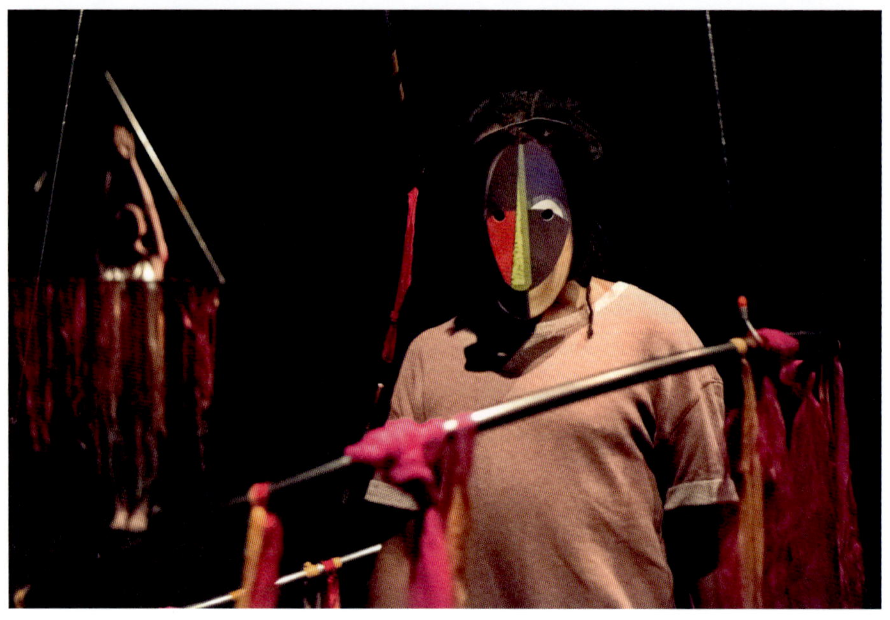

Sonia Boyce, *We move in her way* (production stills), 2016
photography by George Torode

37

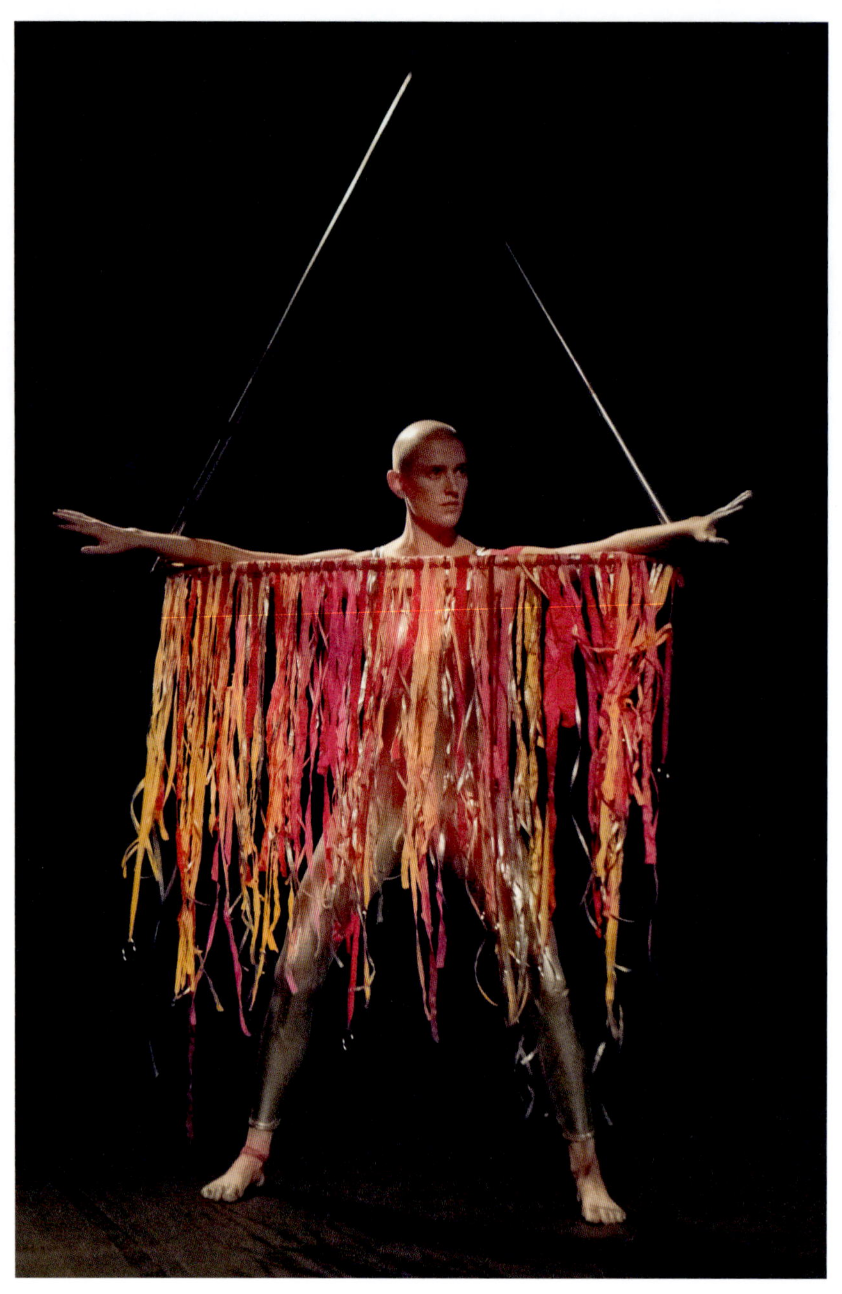

Sonia Boyce, *We move in her way* (production still), 2016
photograph by George Torode

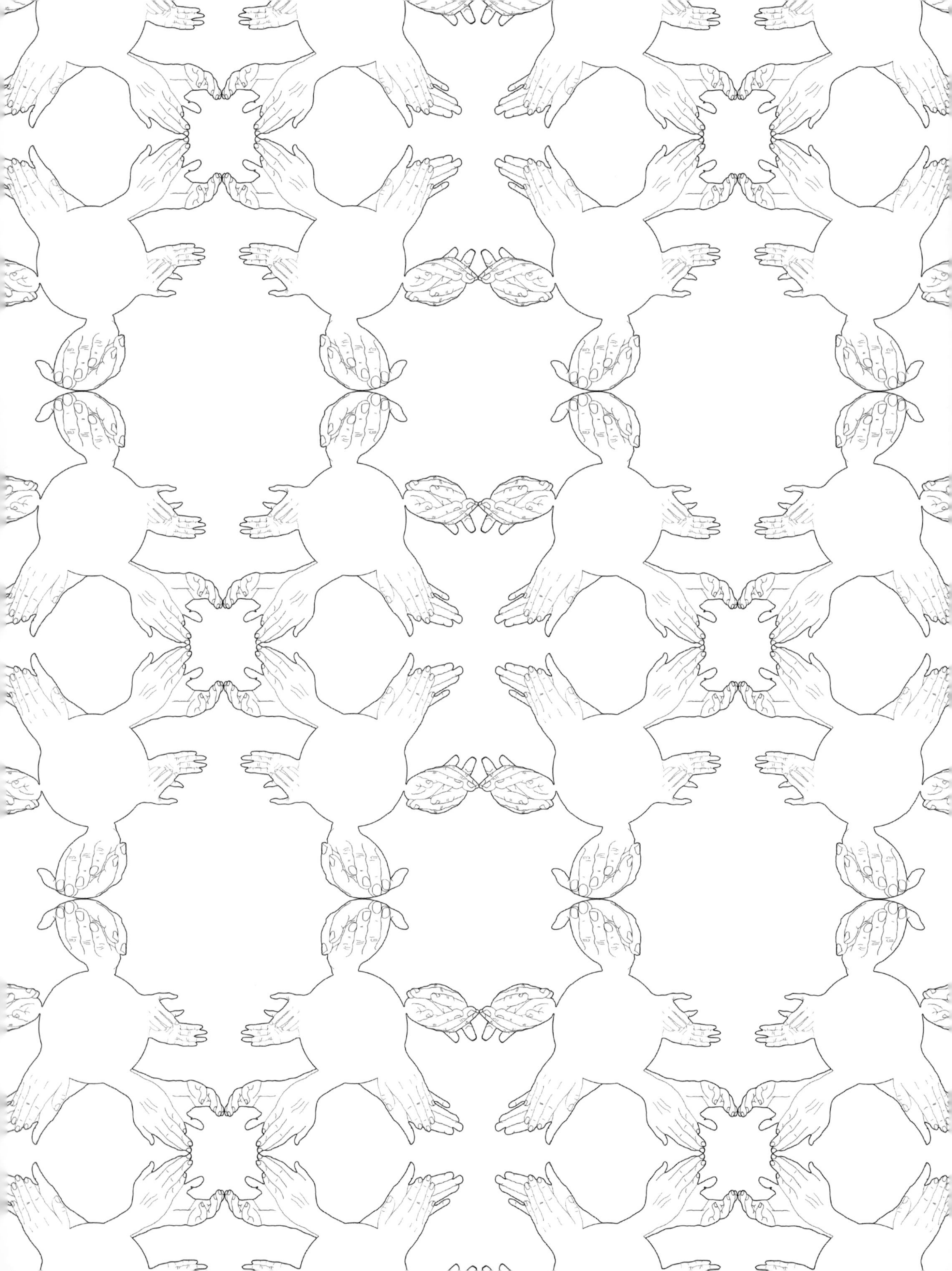

Sonia Boyce, *Clapping Wallpaper 2*, 2024
digital repeat pattern on vinyl, dimensions variable

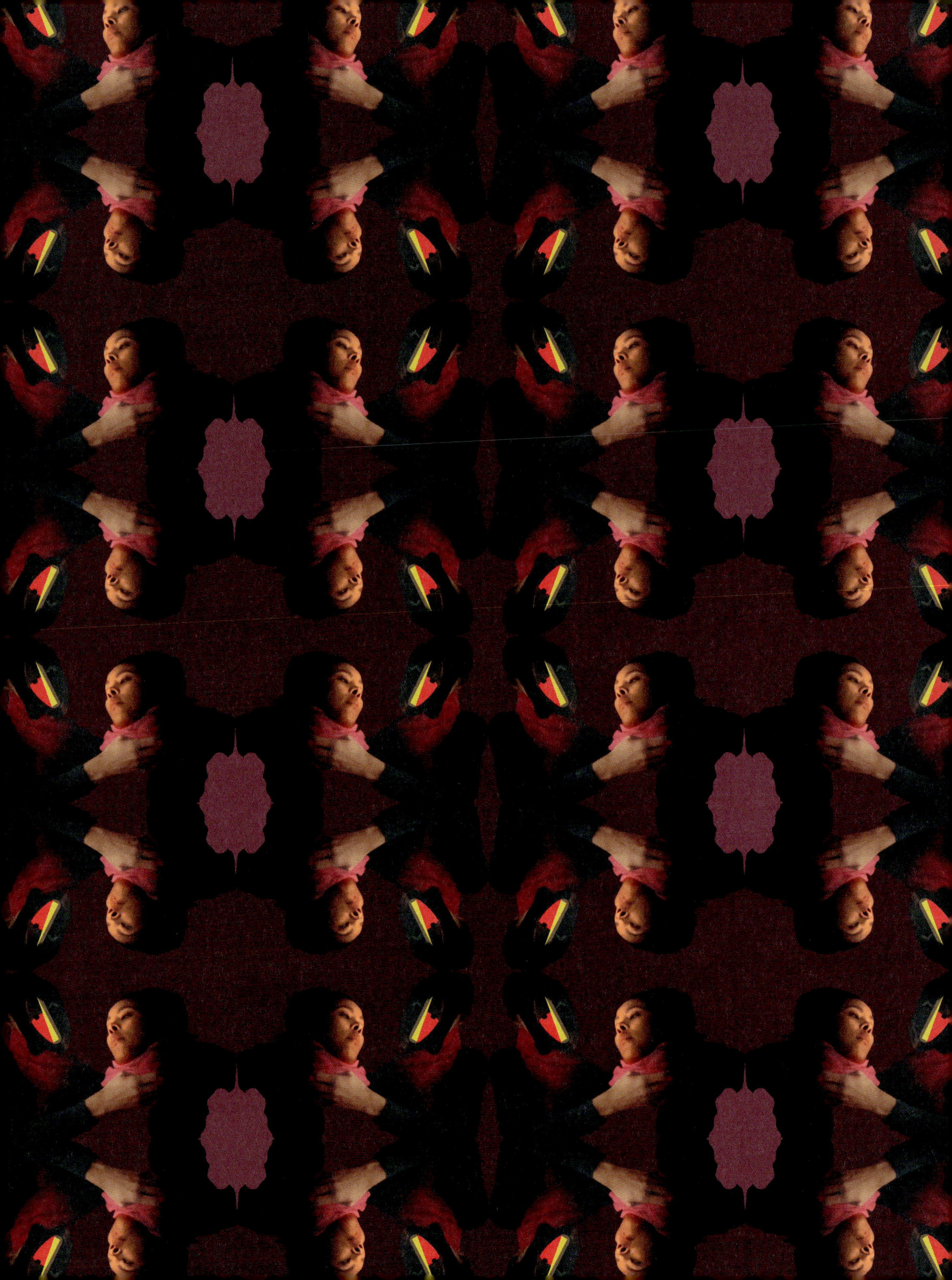

Sonia Boyce, *We move in her way after Lygia Clark and Sophie Taeuber-Arp Wallpaper*, 2017
digital repeat pattern on vinyl, dimensions variable

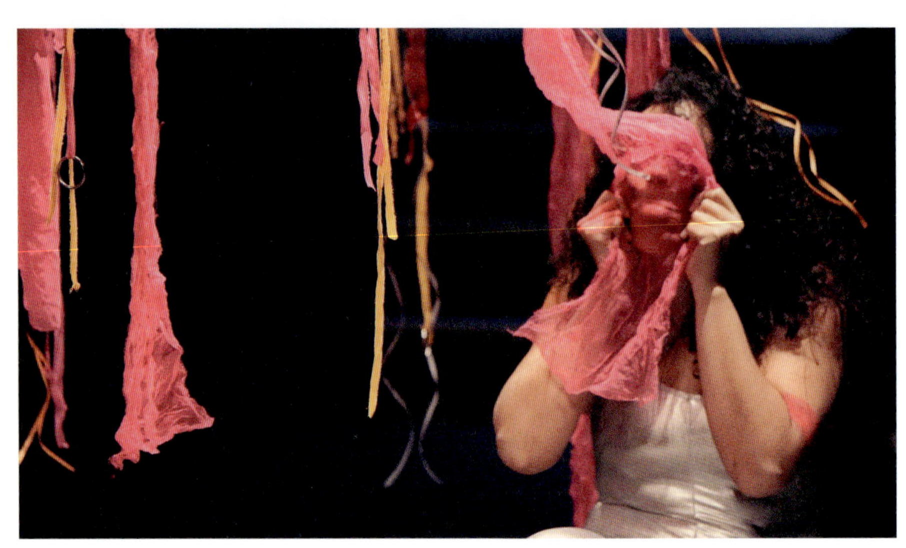

Sonia Boyce, *We move in her way Ria*, 2024
digital print on vinyl, dimensions variable

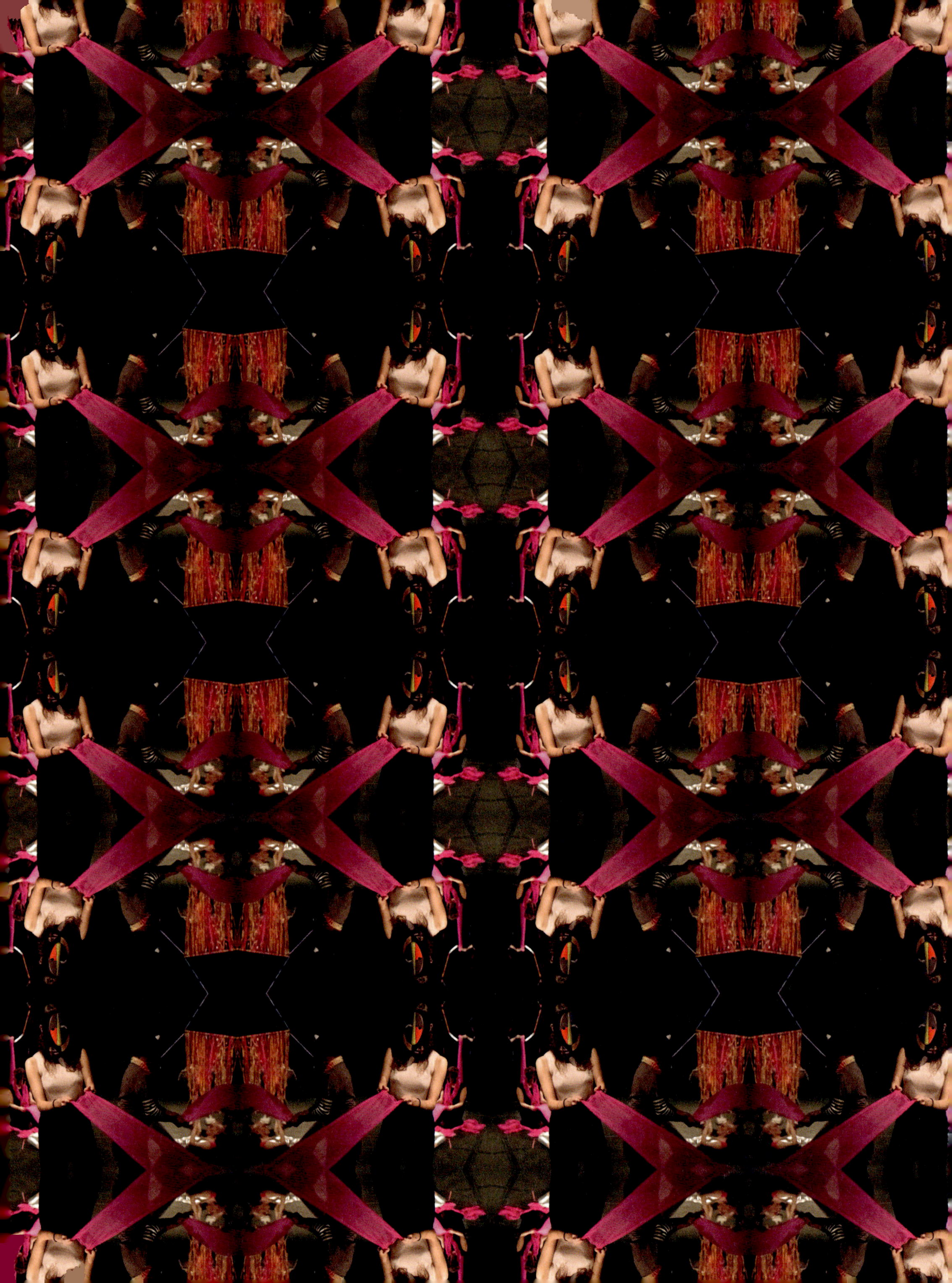

Sonia Boyce, *We move in her way Pattern Audience Wallpaper*, 2017
digital repeat pattern on vinyl, dimensions variable

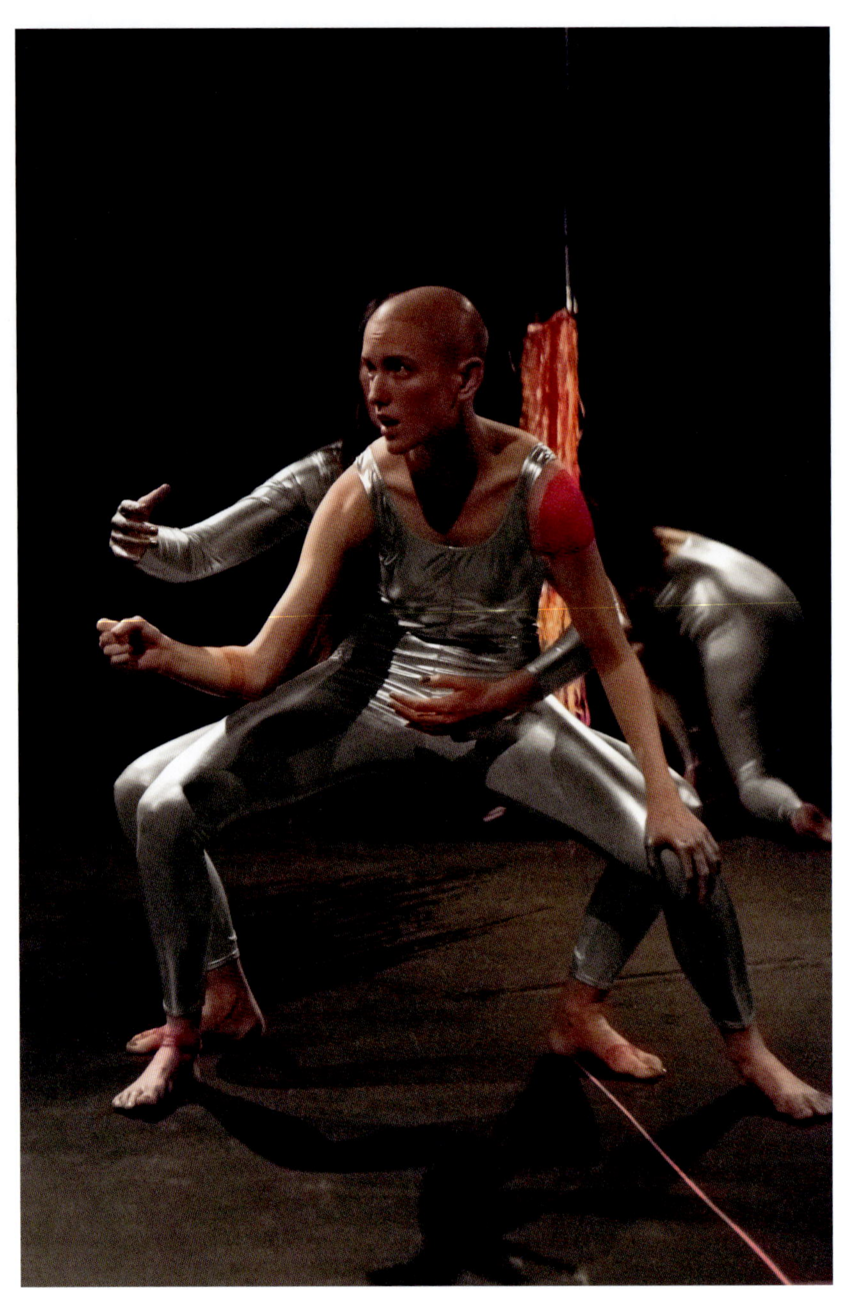

Sonia Boyce, *We move in her way Eve and Be* (production still), 2016
photograph by George Torode

Lygia Clark + Sonia Boyce: A conversation between Michael Asbury, Sonia Boyce and Gilane Tawadros

GILANE TAWADROS (GT)
In the very first issue of the art journal *Third Text*, edited by the artist Rasheed Araeen and published in autumn 1987, there is an essay by the art critic Guy Brett on Lygia Clark entitled 'Lygia Clark: the borderline between art and life'. The essay is preceded by an interview between you, Sonia, and the art critic John Roberts. Your exhibition here at Whitechapel Gallery is entitled 'An Awkward Relation', and the exhibition of Lygia Clark co-curated by you, Michael Asbury and myself is entitled 'Lygia Clark: The I and the You', after a work by Clark from 1967 that is now in the collection of the Museum of Modern Art in New York called *O Eu e o Tu (The I and the You)*. Can we start by talking about the juxtaposition of these two exhibitions and two artists at Whitechapel Gallery, and how the exhibitions came about? Perhaps, Sonia, we could start with you?

SONIA BOYCE (SB)
I'd completely forgotten that the first issue of *Third Text* had both the essay on Lygia Clark and the interview with John Roberts and myself, and in a way it feels like there are several things coming full circle in bringing both Clark's work and my work together. My first encounter with Lygia Clark was through you, Gilane. We were working on a monograph called *Sonia Boyce: Speaking in Tongues* (1997) and you started to talk to me about the hair objects that I was making in the early to mid 1990s. You said that the way in which the works required an activation reminded you of the work of Clark. So that was my first introduction to her work. But I was making these things independently of knowing about her.

I then read about her; got to know her practice; fell in love, of course, as one does. But also, I was making those hair objects at a time in the early 90s when there was a lot of conversation about participation and interaction, without knowing about the historical lineage to someone like Lygia Clark. So, it was my conversations with you, Gilane, that first raised how my work might have a dialogue with Clark's work.

When I was appointed as Director of Whitechapel Gallery in April 2022, my first thought was to reach out to you, Sonia – and subsequently to Michael – to think about how we could present Lygia's work, which hasn't really been seen properly in this country since the 1960s. How could we present the work in a way that was true to – or as close as possible to – Lygia's intentions as an artist. It's important to note that your exhibition at Centre 181 Gallery, London, where you first showed those hair pieces, was titled 'Do You Want to Touch?' (1991). And that could almost be a title of a Lygia Clark exhibition or work.

MICHAEL ASBURY (MA)

I'm quite surprised that that was the first time you were made aware of connections between the participatory nature of your work Sonia, and the precedence of someone like Lygia Clark because you are so close in several different ways. I don't mean formally or even conceptually, but in terms of a specific set of exhibition histories, and in publications such as *Third Text*, as Gilane points out.

However, if we are to speak of precedence, as far as Whitechap-el Gallery is concerned, the idea of a Lygia Clark exhibition here, immediately raises the memory of Hélio Oiticica and his 1969 project-show, 'The Whitechapel Experiment'. We begin therefore with a connection with the 1960s, but also with a set of problems that come with hosting an exhibition of participatory work when an artist is no longer with us.

There are other conversations that arise with past exhibitions such as those at the Hayward Gallery in 1989. 'Art in Latin America' curated by Dawn Ades, and Rasheed Araeen's 'The Other Story: Afro-Asian Art in Post-war Britain'. The former featured work by Lygia Clark, the latter featured your work, Sonia, one of which was used as one of the posters for the show.

Presenting Sonia Boyce and Lygia Clark at the same time at Whitechapel Gallery encourages a conversation about exhibition histories. It reveals how the historical time between the cosmopolitanism of the 1960s and the rising postcolonial approach of the 1980s, was bridged by the work of art critics such as Guy Brett, artists like David Medalla and Rasheed Araeen, as well as in practices such as your own Gilane, with InIVA (Institute of International Visual Arts) which from the 1990s served to weave together these two seemingly distinct artistic trajectories, as well as so many others. To bring together Lygia and Sonia now makes us think about how few those interlocuters were, how the political environment shifted over the course of the 70s, and how incredible it was to see such distinctive groups of artists being discussed side by side, in a journal such as *Third Text*.

GT

What you're saying is very important, Michael. And perhaps we can come back to the need for us to think about different genealogies because there has been a tendency to see artists' practice within very tightly drawn geographical delineations, as well as delineations of time. This prevents us from recognising how artists are influenced and influence each other and intersect with each other in very dynamic ways. This has certainly happened in relation to Latin American art, but it's also happened in relation to the work of black British artists. Despite the very rich diversity of practices, forms and ideas, the work of black British artists remains bound within very tightly delineated art historical definitions.

SB

What's emerging out of the early part of this conversation is the movements and connections of people and their practices. I knew about Guy Brett and David Medalla and Signals gallery – again, through you, Gilane, in terms of the recommissioning of the *Signals* magazine – where one could really dive into these various connections between what was happening in London at a particular moment, but what was also happening across continental Europe and South America.

And, as Michael is suggesting, there were interesting parallels between what was happening in Latin American art and what was emerging among a growing black British artists scene, exemplified by 'The Other Story'. However, at the time – in the 80s – I wasn't fully aware of these possible connections. I was part of a generation that acted like we were the first to come along and challenge the status quo and the story of art as it was being presented. I didn't realise that we were part of a wider geopolitical turn in art.

GT

When I took up my role as the founding Director of InIVA in the early 90s, Guy Brett came to one of the openings very early on. I didn't know him; I didn't know his work except through *Third Text* and his essay on Lygia Clark. He brought me a gift: a copy of the catalogue of his exhibition of Hélio Oiticica at Whitechapel Gallery. And years later, in fact, after Guy died, I reflected that what his gift was signalling to me was the need to be aware that this new organisation InIVA needed to be cognisant of the history of internationalism that preceded it and which had largely been driven by artists and by critics – people like Guy Brett, but also David Medalla, Gustav Metzger and Rasheed Araeen, among others.

There was a big drive to internationalise the contemporary art scene in the 60s, not just in terms of artistic practice, but also in terms of ideas. Going back to Guy's essay on Lygia Clark in *Third Text*, he writes about how it was hard to find Clark's name in the histories of modern sculpture in the late 80s and that it rarely appeared in art magazines at that time. She had, he says, little art market status since the works she had produced after the mid 60s were, in his words, 'virtually unsaleable as art objects'. I'd like to return a bit later to Clark's move away from making conventional artworks to works that are 'virtually unsaleable', but could we start by talking about one of Lygia's first significant exhibitions here in the UK, which was her retrospective at Signals gallery in London in 1965? Can we also talk about the significance of Signals gallery itself in 60s London?

MA

This is very interesting, Gilane, because in the 90s, Guy was fighting for that history to be recognised. He was very upset, for example, with exhibitions such as 'The Sixties Art Scene in London' (1993) at the Barbican Art Gallery. He criticised that show for not reflecting London's true cosmopolitan character during the course of the 60s.[1] It wasn't just Signals that had that international outlook, several London galleries looked beyond Abstract Expressionism and the US Pop art scene, and importantly, Guy also recalled the presence of artists from former British colonies who, although they had been integrated into the various art groupings at the time, have since been largely forgotten.[2]

It is interesting that the internationalism of Signals gallery was very much a product of bureaucratic necessity. Medalla, who as a Filipino needed to regularly renew his visa, found that the easiest way to do so was to live between London and Paris.

This is how the Signals group met Sérgio Camargo, a Brazilian artist who shot to fame after winning the sculpture prize at the 3rd Paris Biennale in 1963. David and Guy, together with Paul Keeler if I'm not mistaken, visited him in Paris and offered him a solo exhibition at Signals. Camargo was a very generous person, and he put Guy and Paul in touch with several other Brazilian artists whom they met in Brazil while Guy, in his capacity as art critic for *The Times*, went to cover the Bienal de São Paulo in 1965.[3] During that trip Guy met Lygia Clark, Mira Schendel and Hélio Oiticica, establishing lifelong friendships with them all.

The interview between Suely Rolnik and Guy is very revealing of the art critic's character. There's a beautiful passage where Guy speaks about meeting Lygia in Rio, when he expresses his desire to buy some work. She said, 'OK, so I'll send you some work by post, don't worry'. Guy talks about receiving a large box in the post full of rubber bands, stones, plastic bags, stuff like that. He recalled, in his measured and calm way of speaking, thinking 'This is really interesting'. It was that initial 'interest', Guy speculates, that gave Lygia the liberty to speak openly to him about her projects and ideas, which were ever more radical.[4]

SB

There are several loops here, but the question about the new or the radically new, particularly within the British art context, and of internationalism predates the 60s. I'm thinking of the Whitechapel Gallery exhibition 'This is Tomorrow' in 1956, which included Den-

is Williams, a Guyanese painter who studied in London, and who has been virtually written out of the historical narrative about that show, despite the exhibition announcing new ways of making and thinking.

The hunger for the new, you could say, seemed to be very important during the mid twentieth century. Yet, when it took place, securing those narratives within an art historical or exhibition histories narrative, occlusion seemed to happen very quickly. We needed someone like Guy Brett in the 60s who embraced art beyond the usual circuits of internationalism at the time, and championed unconventional methods that expanded painting and sculpture.

MA

That's a very important point, Sonia. And you probably don't know, but in the context of my PhD, in the late 90s, I had asked Guy if in the 60s he had been aware of the Independent Group's interest and connections with spectator participation. Guy had said that he was only aware of their connections with Pop art. For me that answer shows how significant details are so quickly forgotten. 'This is Tomorrow' is one of those exhibitions that is remembered, but only partially, mainly in relation to Pop art.

GT

I wonder if I could raise another point here, about another sort of suppression which, Sonia, your comment provokes in my thinking: that of the African presence in Brazilian culture. It is acknowledged in jazz and in Brazilian music of the 1960s. There is an 'African disruption' to ways of seeing, of hearing, of making art and music that enables and facilitates the modernist turn. It's not just Picasso and the impact of African mask-making and his break with artistic conventions. This disruption can also be seen in Brazilian art and literature, and in British art history as well, but remains an unexplored and unwritten – and I don't want to use the word influence because I think it's greater than influence – catalyst. I think it's an intervention and a foundational disturbance that runs beneath these apparently settled histories of modern and contemporary art.

SB

I'm really very happy to be showing *We move in her way* (2017) in this exhibition, because it speaks – very quietly, maybe – about the so called 'influence' of jazz and improvisation on Dada, and Dada's influence on my recent works. It must be remembered that the emergence of jazz across Europe, in the early part of the twentieth century, was generally regarded as the announcement of the modern age – modernism. *We move in her way* is also influenced by some of the exploratory work that Lygia Clark was doing with her students in the Sorbonne in Paris. But it is the question about Dada and art historical accounts of raucous and non-sensical performances that lies at the heart of my enquiry. I am referring to the supposedly anarchic actions that Dadaists sought to develop.

I was thinking about this by revisiting the work of Sophie Taeuber-Arp and the ways in which her costumes and her masks would often refer to African and Pacific-region masks as 'primitive'. The idea of the primitive seemed to be so fundamental; or it was cast as primitive, you could say, in that early modernist moment and the borrowings, the parodying, the tactics of using these so-called 'other' ways of envisaging the world to enrich a European modernist position. *We move in her way* starts to try and work out what's going on in these spaces or these moments that don't necessarily properly bookmark their references and problematic framings.

MA

Dawn Ades wrote a wonderful essay for an exhibition that investigated the proximities or overlaps between Constructivism and Dada in the 1920s.[5] There was something of that overlap which art historian Ronaldo Brito identified in the 'disruptive' side of Neoconcretism which he associated with Lygia Clark, Hélio Oiticica and Lygia Pape.[6] The recurrent and problematic notion of the 'primitive' re-emerges in that context too, particularly in relation to Hélio's involvement with samba and the community of Mangueira in Rio around dance and carnival. Interestingly, according to Guy, both Lygia Clark and the art critic Mario Pedrosa were somewhat critical of the representation of the predominantly black people from Mangueira in Oiticica's 1969 Whitechapel Gallery exhibition catalogue.[7] So, definitely, the presence of Afro-descendent Brazilian culture in the work of those artists, albeit sometimes problematically and in varying degrees of explicitness, is undeniable.

In my opinion, there is an important distinction in the way improvisation is approached in your work, Sonia, compared to the way Lygia Clark approached participation and collaboration. Jean Fisher describes how Sonia allows improvisation and spontaneity to happen by withdrawing at a certain point. Sonia however maintains overall control, according to Fisher, by establishing the initial concept and later determining the form in which the work is presented.[8] You step back at a point, like some directors that welcome improvisation. Later, you return to edit the material and present it to the public. I think that's very distinct from Clark in that you avoid a lot of the problems that arise when showing Clark's work in an exhibition context. With Clark the presence of the artist was fundamental in her process, while not much consideration for 'exhibiting' the participatory work was given. In your case, Sonia, you already envisage a presentation of the work from the start. In this conversation we are bringing up similitudes, connections and so on, but I think we should also emphasise that there are a lot of differences between the two practices. Not only because of the different times, but the different contexts too. These are interrelated and there are crossovers, there are figures and characters that connect or traverse everything, but there are key distinctions to be made.

SB

In the 1980s, there was a repeated question within feminist art practice, but also within black art practice, about audience. Who are you making this for? Who is your audience? And that question of there being this other space – not only in terms of what is made but then who is going to receive what is made – has really influenced me, because it was quite strident, that question, throughout that period. And it still exists today, to a certain extent: the idea that you make something and then there is a receiver of it once it's made.

I'm not speaking of a specific audience, although this was implied during the 80s discourses. What I mean is that the work becomes public and has its publics as soon as it leaves the artist and becomes part of a display or as evidence of a gesture or performative action. To a certain extent I think about the documentation of Lygia Clark's work, and that to document is to imagine another audience.

MA

I don't think documenting her work was so important for Clark. There are notes and letters that have come to largely replace that visual type of documentation. These have become important for us in attempting to remember the work, its significance.

SB

The documentation – and there is plenty of it – probably comes about because of the ephemeral nature of what has taken place and what has been produced and the meanings that have emerged. The documents make me think back to the conversation about Guy Brett receiving the box which he opens and then there are these things. And I assume at a certain point, with Lygia and her practice, that the purpose of documenting was to enable other projects to happen, that documentation allowed people to see what the work was about. I wouldn't want to minimise the question of the documentation because that is its very intention: it envisages a receiver outside of what's actually taking place.

GT

Can we take a step back for a moment and return to the question of the art object as a physical commodity?

Both you, Sonia, and Lygia made a significant move away from making images and objects to making works and interventions premised on social relations and interactions, blurring the line between art and life.

Jean Fisher, as Michael has referenced, wrote about a particular work by you called *For you, only you* (2007) and she likened your role in its making to that of an itinerant troubadour. She said that you occupy 'the uncertain realm of the threshold between self-other relations, where what is at stake is an emancipation and transfiguration of the passage between voicelessness and voice, stranger and neighbour, hostility and hospitality, disempowerment and agency'. Could you reflect on your shift from being an artist making images and art objects to one of a troubadour or producer in the sense that Walter Benjamin[9] used the term and Fisher wrote 'listeners or spectators are not passive consumers of a prescriptive aesthetic or "message", but are empowered by their engaged experience of art?'[10] It would be helpful if you could speak about how *We move in her way* came about: the process of making it and what the audience experiences in that moment of encountering and engaging with the work.

SB

Again, I will go back to the early 90s, when I was in a very transitional period of making. It was quite a radical shift to realise that I didn't want to make self-portraits anymore, that the works were read very much as me marking my identity publicly. I wanted to stop doing that and had to find a way to somehow reach out. This is very fundamental to all the work that I've made since: that I may be present, but the challenge becomes what I might do with others as well as what others might do in the situations that I orchestrate.

I mention the 90s because there was a lot of discussion about what constitutes interaction. I'm not quite sure why interaction became a key rallying call at that moment, but my work shifted in relation to those discussions about not only the self, but also the self and others, and asking others to do things. And then, in that process, documenting them. I suppose realising that, while working with other people, unexpected things occur.

I'm going to speak of a particular work where I'd asked a set of twins whether I could film them kissing. They were both performers and they realised – in the process of filming them – that I didn't know how to direct. I was in this very awkward position where I was working with a project producer, a camera person and a set of twins. I would ask the twins to perform a given action, and they would start, and then they would veer off in all sorts of other directions that I hadn't asked them to do. The situation became very tense because I invited others into the work with the expectation that I would be directing them and then realising that I'm hopeless as a director. Actually, the actions they created out of their own agency were much more interesting than what I was asking them to do. Painful to my ego but, you know, interesting.

It was through this moment that you could say there was a consolidation of lots of different things happening: the question about inviting others into the work and then seeing what transpires, and having to be aware of the power play between egos that often occurs in that context. And actually, having to say, OK, at this point I need to diminish my ego. I want to see what emerges and what other people do. This, I learnt from Lygia Clark: her work in the laboratory setting, what she was doing with the students in Paris, and how a surplus of meanings can arise if you're not trying to override what it is that's unfolding. This became the fundamental way in which I've worked since the 90s, in terms of working with other people and inviting them into a situation and seeing what they do.

What happened at the ICA on the night of the performance of *We move in her way* was that the audience completely took over. There were professional dancers; there were these very ephemeral objects – you know, bits of cloth; there were metal objects and items that were suspended; there were things that could be tapped. And then audience members slowly came into that scenario. They were very nervous at first, but once a few of them started, then they all joined in. The dancers, the crew and everybody else left, and it was just the audience there at the end of the situation. There was an uncertainty about when it was going to finish. The professional performers had been given a set time of about 20 minutes. It went on for nearly two hours. Everybody apart from the audience had packed up and now there was a scenario where nobody was in charge.

Underlying the process, I drew upon the ways in which Lygia Clark worked with her students at the Sorbonne and how she encouraged play to unfold. The students would have a certain exercise that they would carry out and then it would expand, with Lygia encouraging them to voice what they thought was happening as their methods progressed. I love how open that was as a process – how it revealed what was just under the surface of a collective action.

GT

Michael, I wonder if you could reflect on Clark's shift from making geometric, abstract paintings, to thinking about three-dimensional space and planes, and then starting to make participatory works, and the evolution of her practice from that point on?

MA

There is an 'official' version of how this took place that doesn't differ too much from your question, Gilane. It is as if the practice had been predetermined, a teleology of sorts. Such a version – and this is replicated to a similar degree with other 'official' progressions, such as that of Oiticica – describes a gradual shift from the picture frame towards three-dimensional space. I am oversimplifying it here of course, but along the way there was Ferreira Gullar's 1959 'Theory of the Non-Object' that saw in Clark's work a coming together of the fields of painting and sculpture, which was then further confirmed by her articulated geometric sculptures in the form of the *Bichos*.[11] From the early 60s onwards, a noticeable incorporation of ephemeral materials began, with the action *Caminhando* (1963) and the matchbox constructions the following year, for example. Clark then started to loosen her reliance on geometrical form and became more interested in the relationship between the participant and the object, the actor, the action and what this might unleash, subjectively. Her former rigour remained throughout, of course. Nevertheless, I believe this is not the most interesting way in which to describe the transition, with Clark, or with any

other artist from her generation. There is something that the collective brings to the table, so to speak, that is far more interesting and richer than the sum of the individual achievements. How her practice progressed in relation to her peers, how they complemented each other seems to me more interesting.

SB

I don't actually know how she transitioned from making these constructivist works to the relational works. Do you know why or how that happened?

MA

I think what encouraged her to use objects that invited experiential experimentation was her reading of several psychoanalytic theories. Donald Winnicott and his study of transitional objects, for example: objects that children become attached to as a means of reassurance and so on, bits of cloth, teddies, pillows, that kind of thing. This influenced her and set the foundations for her ephemeral objects, the stone held by the air in a bag, the elastic bands that are stretched by the placement of two pebbles, and later, the work with the students in Paris, which fed into her individual therapy sessions that she considered no longer as art, per se, but as having a healing aspect, forms of psychological care. She positioned these objects in relation to the patient's body according to the person's malaise. So, a gradual transition took place. And I guess there was an abandonment of art, if you understand art in a particular way, as an art object and so forth. She became more and more interested in the bodily experience: how one experiences one's own body and how one's own body communicates, informs, past trauma, and so on.

Her gaze moved inwards in this sense, while someone like Oiticica sought experiential practices, positions and so forth that were more outward-looking. The difficulty he had in getting his plan for his 1969 Whitechapel 'Experience' related to the fact that the emphasis was no longer on discrete objects but on environments. This is why their work is so often considered side by side, and the metaphor of the glove is used: Hélio is the outside of the glove and Lygia is the inside. I don't think you can pinpoint – as in Sonia's case – a particular moment in Clark's work when that transition happened. I think it was a gradual thing. There was her interest in the ephemerality of the object – plastic bags, stones, elastic bands – and that is something that happened in conjunction with an artist like Oiticica, as well as with

Lygia Pape, who was also using very common materials to create work. But at some moment Clark became interested in psychoanalytic theories, how objects relate to oneself and this became all the more explicit in the work particularly during her years in Paris, from 1968 to 1976.

SB

We mustn't forget that, particularly by the end of the 60s and into the 70s, art critics like Lucy Lippard were already alerting us to the dematerialisation of the art object.[12] This was happening in the wider context of debates about the limits of what can be art. What constitutes the activity of art? The artwork in its 'proper' and 'conventional' sense was under intense scrutiny by the 60s. And I'm not just talking about the influence of Marcel Duchamp, here.

GT

In the post-war period, there was a challenge to the commodification of the art object and to what constituted an artwork, but there were tendencies that also seemed to be going in the opposite direction, with Pop art and with artists like Jasper Johns, Robert Rauschenberg and Andy Warhol, for example.

You had artists who were embracing an emerging consumer culture and the possibility of a democratisation of art and of an elision between the objects of everyday life and what constituted an artwork on the one hand, and on the other you had a challenge to the commodification of everyday life and a desire to slow things down. During a period of rapid technological progress, Lygia Clark was making works about touch and physical sensation and working with ephemeral and hand-made materials, not things that were highly wrought and manufactured. She was also incorporating natural objects like stones into her work, and many of the objects she was making before she moved into the more participatory and ephemeral works have a sense of being natural and organic.

SB

I do think this is where I diverge from the coupling that could be imagined between myself and Lygia, in that all the works I make are highly fabricated. They use industrial processes; they use man-made materials like synthetic hair. I purchase things to become part of the work. I'm very aware of the representations, you could say, of body parts in my work. And the language of my work probably aligns more closely to that of Warhol or any of those other artists that look at the consumable object, rather than using things directly from nature, or detritus objects almost rejected as consumable. Lygia used objects that were manufactured but were also understood as detritus without value, such as plastic bags, whereas I work more closely within the realm of representation, and an acute awareness of the mediation of representation, than I think Lygia did. I am more influenced by post-structuralist ideas of deconstructing mainstream forms of representation, although more recent thinking has challenged the binary nature of post-structuralist discourse.

MA

Lygia loved the netting that is used for packaging fruit, as well as plastic bags and elastic bands: things that usually hold the actual commodity. But also, something that comes out from the Suely Rolnik interviews – particularly her conversation with Yve-Alain Bois – is emphasis on the fact that Clark arrived in Paris just after May 68 and that a politically charged atmosphere was still very much part of the scene.[13]

Sonia mentioned Lucy Lippard and the notion of the dematerialisation of art. Lippard was extraordinary in how she was able to capture, to sense perhaps would be a better word, how contemporary art was shifting during those final years of the 60s in New York. Yet, such a narrative also overshadows other trajectories, other means of arriving at similar conclusions, whether formal or conceptual. Clark is an excellent example in this respect. When she arrived in Paris, in the wake of May 68 and all that that entailed, a special dossier on her work was published in *Robho*, an independent journal edited by Jean Clay. That edition of *Robho* featured the 'guerilla tactics' of black theatre groups in the US while on its cover, it featured the image of 200-metre sprinter Tommie Smith, standing on the podium at the 1968 Mexico City Olympics with his right arm raised in the Black Power fist in solidarity with the civil rights movement (and perhaps also the victims of Mexican police repression in the days preceding the event's opening).[14]

Later that same year, Clay travelled to Argentina where he was invited to be a member of an art prize jury together with Lippard. It was during that trip, and the first-hand experience of the radicalism of a group of artists in Rosario and Buenos Aires who led the Tucumán Arde happenings and event, that to a large extent informed Lippard's notion of dematerialisation of art on the one hand, and, on the other, further consolidated Clay's move away from kineticism and towards ever more

political stances in relation to art practices.[15] I would imagine that such a shift in outlook towards art and culture was in the air, whether in Buenos Aires, New York, Paris or London.

So, what I am trying to argue is that, although Clark wasn't overtly political, she was certainly part of a greater artistic milieu undergoing profound political radicalisation as was the case with Guy and Medalla in London, Oiticica in Rio and so forth. As argued by Yve-Alain Bois, Clark was entirely aware that her workshops with the students at the Sorbonne were a direct consequence of May 68, and the increasing radicalism of her work, while not overtly political, was certainly enabled by the wider politicised scene.[16] Despite the increasing repressive regime in Brazil, some student and general manifestations also took place that year, amongst them 'The March of the One Hundred Thousand'. In the field of culture, despite government censorship, or arguably because of it, an incredible cross-disciplinary, intermedia if you like, 'movement' that had begun in the early 60s consolidated around the year 1967. It brought artists, poets, musicians and film-makers together in a fervent cultural environment most famously encapsulated by the term *Tropicália*.[17]

SB
So again, I'll go back to the 90s and into the early 2000s. One of the ongoing discussions within performance art was about the document and its relationship to the performance. I'm very much working from the position of an interface, you could say, where there seemed to be a tension between the performance and its documentation. What do you give weight to? Is the document a secondary item, a poor relation somehow, to the performative moment? And is it really something that just goes into the archive? Or is it a thing? I'm often asked which one is more important. Is it the action that emerges in these encounters? Or is it the documentation – and then what you do with it? As if there is a split.

I think that the moment that you document something, it becomes a thing – an object in the world. Whether it becomes a thing only of that moment, or whether it becomes a thing that then goes off into another realm of its own importance, is up for grabs.

The nature, or possibilities of the documented moment, might not have been a point of discussion when Lygia was augmenting her situations with other people and creating the artworks. But because of the archival turn in contemporary art that has given the document its prominence, we must think about it as both an archival trace as well as an object that lives on – it enters other systems of circulation and meaning. It's not an irrelevance, or necessarily to be treated with reverence. And, of course, it poses many questions for the very nature of the exhibition that we're putting together.

GT
In talking about the work and its documentation and the idea of detritus and what is valueless, you raise two important points that we should touch on. The first is that, it seems to me, one cannot separate the discussion of what is the work and what is the document, from the art market and the valuation of work. By which I mean the financial valuation of a work and how it enters the market. In recent years, there have been debates within museums and also in commercial galleries and auction houses about whether the document constitutes a work and therefore accrues financial value, especially when the artist is no longer alive.

So, I wonder if we could talk about this question of value and the post-commodification of works that seems to go against the artist's intention, which is against the grain of that commodification and financial valuation.

The second question is about how these works enter the museum and how – one of the things we've tussled with in curating Lygia's exhibition – we stay true to her intentionality and the feel of her early exhibitions at the 34th Venice Biennale in 1968 and earlier at Signals gallery in London. The artist intended the works to be touched and interacted with, so going against the mandate of the contemporary art museum to conserve and preserve the art object, which is of great financial value. Clark's *Bichos,* matchboxes and other works are therefore placed in cases where they can't be touched. In fact, this is precisely the opposite of an invitation to touch.

MA

I have an anecdote that relates to this. I was visiting a show – my memory is a bit hazy, probably 'Century City' at Tate Modern in 2001 – with David Medalla, when he saw a *Bicho* by Lygia Clark. And at the time you weren't allowed to touch them, but they weren't yet placed within acrylic cases either. David proceeded to articulate the *Bicho*, much to the alarm of the gallery invigilators. He then gave a lecture about the participatory nature of the artwork and how Lygia Clark's work was groundbreaking in that respect. Every-one stopped to listen, invigilators included, given David's incredible story telling abilities.

The Lygia Clark estate under-stands that reproductions of the works are necessary because, otherwise, the work is vastly re-duced. It becomes a static object and completely misrepresents the very nature of the work and the artist's purpose.

As curators we are now in a more fortunate position in the sense that we can use reproduc-tions of works such as the *Bichos* allowing manipulation still to take place. However, as far as Clark's entire oeuvre is concerned, this only solves the problem partially. The collective practices, the work-shop-like sessions, that she organ-ised in Paris with the students – precisely the ones that impressed Sonia so much – have continued despite Clark's absence in the work of mentees Lula Wanderley and Gina Ferreira. However, these rightly take place in non-exhibi-tion contexts. As an art practice that existed on the very limits of art, such works may be now ir-retrievable, remembered only through documentation. The dif-ference between document and artwork now distinguishes Clark's participatory exercises from So-nia's practice.

In the case of Lygia Clark, once the artist is no longer present, we risk betraying the nature of the work, presenting a memory that is (re)constituted through photographs, hearsay and the occasional film footage. These incidental vestiges that document, that come to represent Clark's work are very different from Sonia's practice, which incorporates the documentation of the action within the production of the work, through the post-production of the participatory stage. Sonia, having emerged as an artist alongside the so-called 'archival-turn', incorporates the documentation as an integral element in her process.

SB

There are still legacy issues, you could say, relating to the works that I make. But you know, I do think that at the heart of this endeavour we're exploring in this exhibition is the conundrum between the original and the copy, and the copy somehow belonging to the sphere of the archive. If these objects – I'm talking specifically about Lygia's work here – were meant to be just one-to-one encounters that nobody else was paying any attention to, the very nature of putting them on display starts to create something other than the artist's intention. However, in her lifetime she did show work. She made the works and sanctioned their documentation. Therefore, this be-

comes a very grey area. This is not an either/or scenario. The question is to what extent was Lygia interested in the publicness of what she was doing? Fundamentally, this is a question about the copy and the original. I'm talking both about the literal bodily encounter and its documentation, as well as reproducing works that are meant for encounter. This is an absolute conundrum and we are investing in that conundrum by doing this project.

GT

And to a certain extent we're creating a mass spectator experience, where Lygia Clark's work really encourages a very intimate, almost solitary encounter and engagement between just a couple of people or a handful of people.

MA

Having said all that, Lygia was by no means consistent in terms of the presentation of her work. In Suely Rolnik's interview with Suzana de Moraes, the subject of a party comes up, where Rolnik attempted to introduce Lygia Clark to the psychoanalyst Félix Guattari. A slide projection with images of Clark's sessions with the groups of students was set up – but the whole idea was a complete failure. In the end, Guattari didn't pay attention to the slides and those at the party who did, mocked and laughed at those exercises. According to Moraes, Lygia was very upset and hurt by the whole experience.

The anecdote serves as a warning of sorts for curators seeking to showcase the work of Lygia Clark. There is an expectation that comes with art historical recognition. One that assumes that Clark's work could be exhibited or shown, and that people would naturally interact or relate to it through the aid of documentation and or exhibitions copies. So, yes, the question of intimacy and the public realm, remains a conundrum. There were incidents, for example, when Lygia herself refused to show her work if it wasn't going to be open to participation, when a museum or gallery was only interested in the work as 'objects' of art.[18] As you said, Sonia, it's a grey area.

SB

There are several things that I get from what you're saying, Michael. One is that I absolutely and genuinely believe she thought that what she was doing was incredibly important, and that she wanted to share the importance through displaying the work. What does it mean to encounter the world with others, with objects? Why is this therapeutic? It's a term that, within the visual arts, we are very uncom-

fortable with. The idea that somehow an artwork can do you good, can open a productive and positive space during the encounter. I absolutely believe she was very genuine in the seriousness of that endeavour, to bring people into a sensory awareness of themselves and others in the world, as well as the fact that she was augmenting these encounters with her own ego. I'm not using the term ego as something detrimental, but something that is a fundamentally human experience, to be taken seriously and to be engaged with.

I can see how the representation of the works through documentation and the actual encounter amount to a very different sensory experience. The moment that those encounters were documented, she wanted them out there in the world, as far as I'm concerned. It was not only about what happened in the therapeutic room between counsellor and whoever was receiving that therapeutic experience. She wanted them out in the world. Whether there was then a thought-through discussion about what that meant is another thing.

That's why I mentioned that in the 90s there were strong discussions – which are still being played out now – about which is the most important thing. The performance or its documentation? This is why there was a fierce discussion within the field of performance about Marina Abramovic reperforming not only her own works but also those of other artists. Some performance artists absolutely refuse to document their work because they want it to be experienced only in that sensorial moment of it happening – in the here and now – and not to have an afterlife and not, as Gilane is asking us, to be commodified in a particular way.

This will remain a conundrum for a very long time, but it's a conundrum that continues to ask many more questions, I think. I'm not sure that we're here to answer those questions specifically, but it sits as a cornerstone in what we're trying to do.

MA

I think we can understand this historiographically. Back in the 1960s – whether here or especially in Brazil – the art market was much smaller than it is today, so these issues were not as significant or important for an artist. Of course there was a desire to 'live from one's art' in whatever form that might take, but things were very different if compared with today's art market that is ready to devour everything in its way. What I am trying to say is that alongside that radical, utopian, absolute belief in one's art practice, there was also a certain innocence in terms of what exactly would be commodified and what could not.

SB

I would also add, in terms of the question of the art market, that artists do have to live. They must pay their bills; they must find the money to make the work. And if one speaks of Lygia Clark and the importance not only of the market that may have been in Brazil, but that may also have been in Paris, that may have been in other parts of the UK or anywhere in the world, we are speaking about what it is that enabled her and any other artist – including myself – to continue to make works. Because making work is not cheap. I can fully understand the need to commodify, to monetise an activity, and how she may have gone into the therapeutic field for very pragmatic reasons as much as for creative, intellectual and profoundly human reasons. Artists don't live outside of an economic system.

MA

Lygia Clark was a wealthy woman from an upper-class or bourgeois background, as most of the artists in that milieu had to be to be able to afford a career. It would have been difficult to survive as an artist in Brazil at the time, and possibly to a large extent to this day. Arguably, the art market has enabled artists from different social backgrounds to practise more recently. This is not to say that she didn't have her own financial difficulties and make huge sacrifices, particularly during her time in Paris.[19]

GT
This conversation about the economic context in which artists can and can't make work is very important.

MA
I'd like to add that Lygia Clark's move towards therapy represents the closing of a full circle according to some narratives that claim the constructivist-oriented vanguards in Brazil, and especially in Rio, emerged from the experience of art therapy, with artists and critics participating in workshops at the Pedro II psychiatric hospital at Engenho de Dentro in Rio during the late 1940s. I mention this in my essay in this catalogue. Lygia's assistants Lula Wanderley and Gina Ferreira continued working with her method until very recently, in a clinical setting, at the hospital where all this started in the 40s. So, there is a legacy in Brazil that, in relation to psychiatry dates back to the 1930s, of art transcending its own field, within which Lygia is an important part.

SB
Similarly, in terms of the UK context, cultural studies – particularly figures like Stuart Hall – and media studies have had a huge impact on my generation of practitioners. Art school and my art school education at the end of the 70s and into the early 80s was dominated by Greenbergian theory in terms of art practice.[20] But there was a parallel universe, you could say, where cross-disciplinary discussions were emerging through the practice of cultural theory because it was looking at images and strategies of representation.

This also adds to what is being said about the slightly wider context: transdisciplinary thinking and, for me, feminist theory and cultural studies, and out of that, media studies, which is now quite commonplace within the art school. But when I was at art school that was not the case. Those discussions were happening in another independent space that fuelled a lot of the practice that developed in the 80s and onwards.

GT
I wonder if we could finish by talking about the relevance of Lygia Clark now and why it is important to present these two projects together at Whitechapel Gallery in 2024?

SB

For myself, I think that the shift that is being made by bringing these two ways of working together – and this may sound punitive – is to give the audience work to do. There is a call not to be a passive receiver. And I don't truly believe, actually, that when one goes into galleries and museums one is a passive receiver. We are asking those who come into the gallery space to pay attention to the work and themselves. Work for the eyes. Work to move. Work to connect, to engage not only at a voyeuristic distance. And I'm thinking about my first encounter with Lygia Clark's work, which was at Whitechapel Gallery in a show by Catherine de Zegher called 'Inside the Visible' (1996).

In the upper gallery at Whitechapel, Lygia's work was exhibited where my work is going to be shown. There was a massive, low-level plinth, upon which there were many different objects. And there was something that occurred that's very hard to describe, in picking up these objects and playing with them. It took me back to a moment of childhood when you could pick up a comb and it becomes a microphone. You imagine it as something else. It taps into the imagination in a particular way that is very theatrical. And then you put it back down and it resumes being a mundane object. But the moment that you pick it up, these imaginings occur. I found it very curious that picking up an inert object in a gallery space could tap into my imagination in that way.

GT

That's beautiful. Michael?

MA

I'm glad Catherine de Zegher and Stuart Hall are mentioned because they represent intellectual strands that intersect here. I think that these two exhibitions we are currently organising bring together forgotten transnational connections, interconnected art histories as well as distinct yet corresponding narratives of struggle. They recall historical struggles of representation, whether we think of them in terms of feminism, black culture in the UK, international neo-avant-gardes, postcolonial and decolonial turns or, indeed, the conjunction of all of these.

1. Guy Brett, 'The Sixties Art Scene in London', *Third Text*, vol. 7, issue 23 (1993) 121–23.

2. Ibid.

3. For a discussion on Sergio Camargo and Brett & Keeler's meeting with Mira Schendel in 1965, see Michael Asbury, 'Sergio Camargo: E Agora Jose?', in *Encontros Fundamentais, IAC 20 Anos*, ed. Jacopo Criveli Visconti (São Paulo: Instituto de Arte Contemporanea, 2020) 22–63.

4. Interview with Guy Brett, *Suely Rolnik: Archive pour une œuvre-événement – Projet d'activation de la mémoire corporelle d'une trajectoire artistique et son contexte* [DVD] ed. Suely Rolnik (Paris: Carta Blanca Editions, 2010). A collection of twenty interviews on the subject of Lygia Clark and spectator participation.

5. Dawn Ades, 'The Janus Face of the Twenties', in *Dada – Constructivism* (exh. cat.) (London: Annely Juda Fine Art, 1984) 35.

6. Ronaldo Brito, *Neoconcretismo: Vértice e Ruptura do Projeto Construtivo Brasileiro* (Rio de Janeiro: Marcos Marcondes, 1975).

7. Guy Brett, 'Untitled statement', in *Oiticica in London,* eds. Guy Brett & Luciano Figueiredo (London: Tate Publishing, 2007) 11–16, 14.

8. Jean Fisher, 'For you, only you: The Return of the Troubadour', in *For you, only you: A Project by Sonia Boyce*, ed. Paul Bonaventura (exh. cat.) (Oxford: Ruskin School of Drawing & Fine Art, Oxford University, 2007) 42–51.

9. Walter Benjamin, 'The Author as Producer', in *Reflections*, trans. Edmund Jephcott (New York: Schocken Books, 1986) 233–237.

10. Fisher, op cit., 1.

11. Ferreira Gullar, 'Theory of the Non-Object', in *Suplemento Dominical, Jornal do Brasil* (19–20 December 1959). English translation in: Michael Asbury (ed.), *Neoconcrete Experience* (exh. cat.) (London: Gallery 32, Brazilian Embassy, 2009).

12. Lucy Lippard, *Six Years: The Dematerialization of the Art Object from 1966 to 1972* (originally published, New York: Praeger, 1973; annotated edition republished, Berkeley: University of California Press, 1997).

13. Rolnik, op. cit., Interview with Yve-Alain Bois.

14. *Robho*, no.4 (October 1968).

15. Such a shift is clearly perceptible in the subsequent double-edition, see *Robho* no.5–6 (December 1971).

16. According to Yve-Alain Bois, the very possibility of holding those types of workshops at the Sorbourne would have been impossible had the students not rebelled against the conservatorism of the institution a few months prior to the artist's arrival. See Rolnik, op. cit., Interview with Yve-Alain Bois.

17. Originally an installation by Oiticica, its title being appropriated by Caetano Veloso for an emerging music genre with repercussions in theatre and cinema.

18. Rolnik, op. cit., Interview with Yve-Alain Bois.

19. Luciano Figueiredo (ed.), *Lygia Clark, Hélio Oiticica: Cartas 1964–74* (2nd edição) (Rio de Janeiro: Editora UFRJ, 1998).

20. Clement Greenberg, *Art and Culture: Critical Essays* (Boston: Beacon Press, 1965).

72

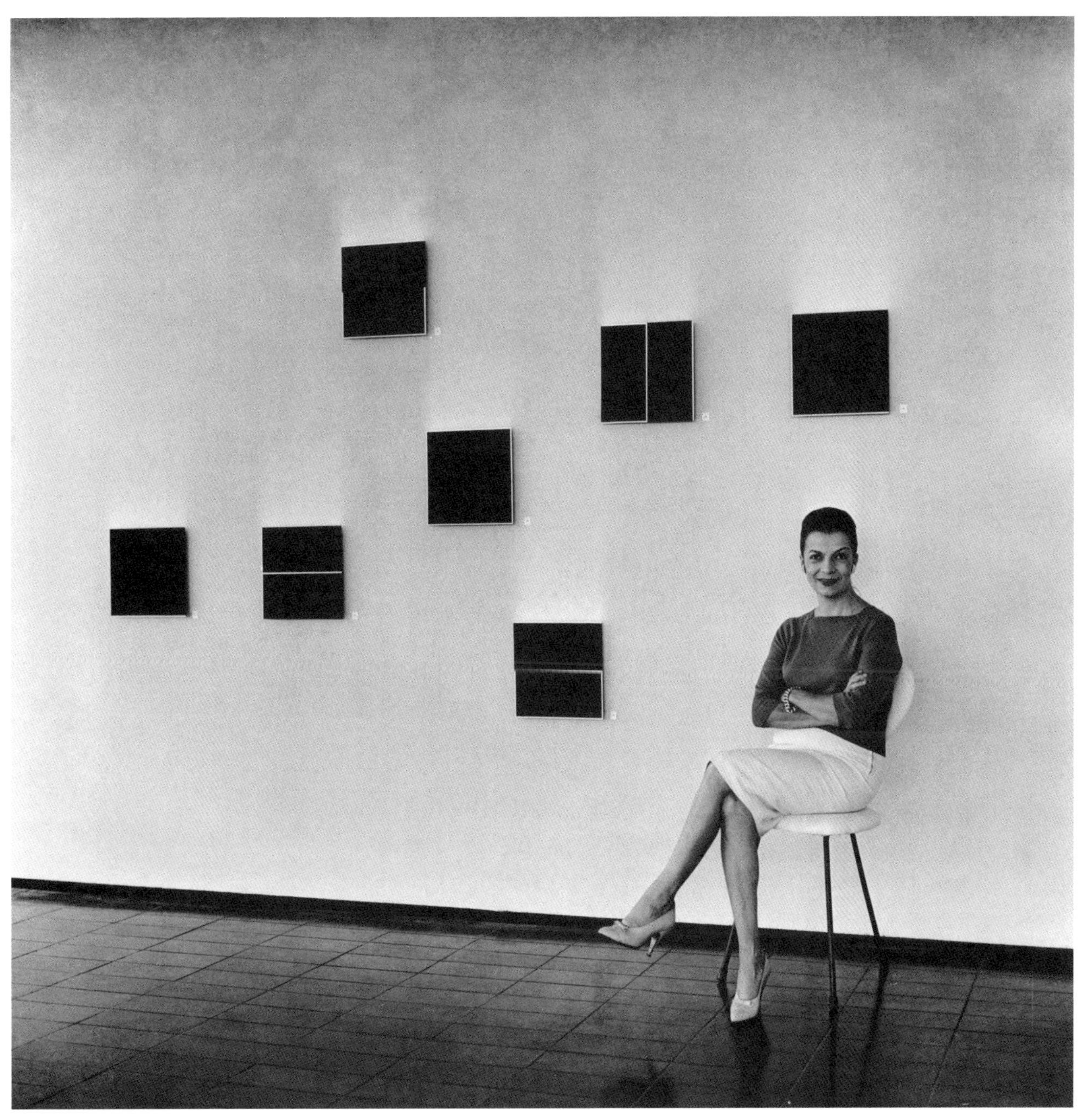

Lygia Clark with her *Unidades*, at the 'Neoconcrete Exhibition', MAM, Rio de Janeiro, 1959
courtesy Associação Cultural O Mundo de Lygia Clark

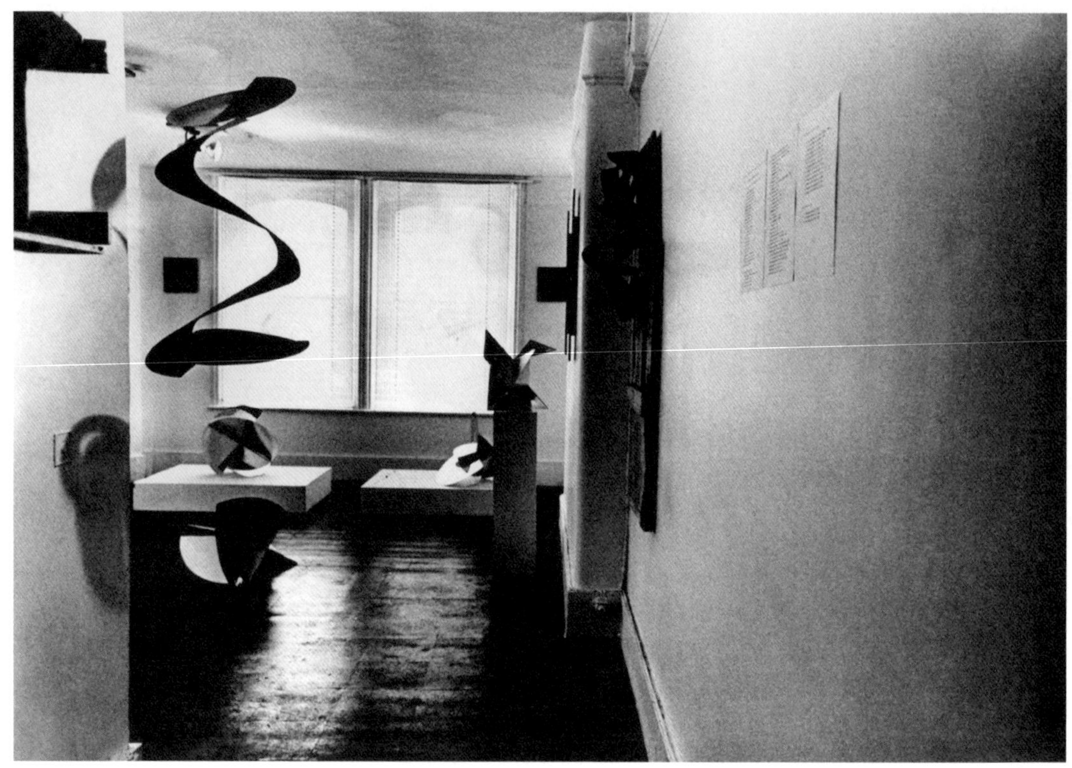

Installation shot from Lygia Clark's exhibition at Signals, London, 1965
photograph by Clay Perry, courtesy Associação Cultural O Mundo de Lygia Clark

Big Woman Talk: Entanglements Between the Work of Lygia Clark and Sonia Boyce

The exhibition 'Lygia Clark: The I and the You' covers a cross-section of the artist's oeuvre, from her abstract geometrical paintings of the 1950s to her collective participatory practice developed with students at the Sorbonne in Paris. The exhibition's title is taken from Clark's own *O Eu e o Tu* (1967) which she produced shortly before leaving for France, where she would live until 1976. *The I and the You* marks a pivotal moment in the artist's career. It stood between her use of discrete objects, increasingly ephemeral in nature, that invited participation or activation, and proposals for the collective actions that took place in the post-May-1968 scenario at the Sorbonne. Those group sessions would inform much of her subsequent *Structuring of the Self* therapy work, which she carried out until her death in 1988.

Clark's *O Eu e o Tu* consists of two full bodysuits that resemble protective work gear.[1] They isolate the wearers from external stimuli, focusing on the relational possibilities of touch. As the suits are connected via a type of umbilical cord, one is encouraged to search and explore the other. Gendered shapes and forms, orifices and protuberances, are revealed by opening pockets concealed by zippers on the opposite suit. Tania Riveira has argued that with *O Eu e o Tu*, Clark 'vigorously entangles and disrupts the traditional equations between sex and gender, destabilizing and shaking the dominant discourse on identity and anatomical references'.[2]

By naming the exhibition 'The I and the You', the work gains here yet another interpretation. The interstitial space that it proposes between self and other – which Clark would call 'relational' after her readings of psychoanalytical studies by Pierre Fédida and Donald Winnicott, among others – is transposed onto a wider historiographical plateau. Clark's practice is presented within the exhibition as a discrete, diverse and complex body, while it also critically, and perhaps provocatively, overflows into the adjacent gallery space, intersecting with the exhibition dedicated to Sonia Boyce's work. Entitled 'An Awkward Relation', it features works to be touched and video installations stemming from participatory and improvisatory settings that Boyce has activated.

Two distinct exhibitions thus intersect in a shared third space, a physical and metaphorical place, where the work of one speaks to that of the other across time. Productively anachronistic, this dialogue traces the distinct paths of each artist while relating one to the other. If this idea sounds farfetched, it might help to remember that Clark proposed something similar in her posthumous letter to Mondrian:

> Today I feel more solitary than yesterday. I feel an enormous need to look at your work, old and also solitary. I came across you in a fabulous photo and felt as if you were here with me, and then I didn't feel so alone. Maybe tomorrow I can also give of my eyes, of my solitude of my persistence to someone who will be an artist like me or perhaps even like you.[3]

Between 1947 and 1948, Clark studied with Roberto Burle Marx, Brazil's foremost modernist garden designer and Purism-inspired painter. She later attended Fernand Léger's academy in Paris between 1950 and 1951. Upon her return to Brazil, she participated in several exhibitions including the second São Paulo Biennial in 1953. The following year Clark became a founding member of the Grupo Frente in Rio de Janeiro, a loose gathering of artists under the leadership of Ivan Serpa, whose admiration of Piet Mondrian, Josef Albers and Kazimir Malevich, among others, would set the foundations for the emergence of the Neoconcrete group later that decade.

According to Yve-Alain Bois, who befriended the artist upon her arrival in Paris in 1968, Clark's own take on the European avant-gardes was idiosyncratic to say the least. On one occasion, Clark had argued, much to the future art historian's surprise, that she considered Mondrian and Albers, crucial influences in her early abstract geometric work, respectively as an iconoclast and a surrealist of sorts.[4] Similarly, Clark's early interest in the intersection of painting and architectural form cannot solely explain the trajectory that her practice took over the course of the 1960s and beyond.

Evidencing, in so many ways, Brazil's seeming irrevocable self-confidence, the 'Neoconcrete Manifesto' was published in Rio de Janeiro in the pages of the weekend supplement of the daily broadsheet

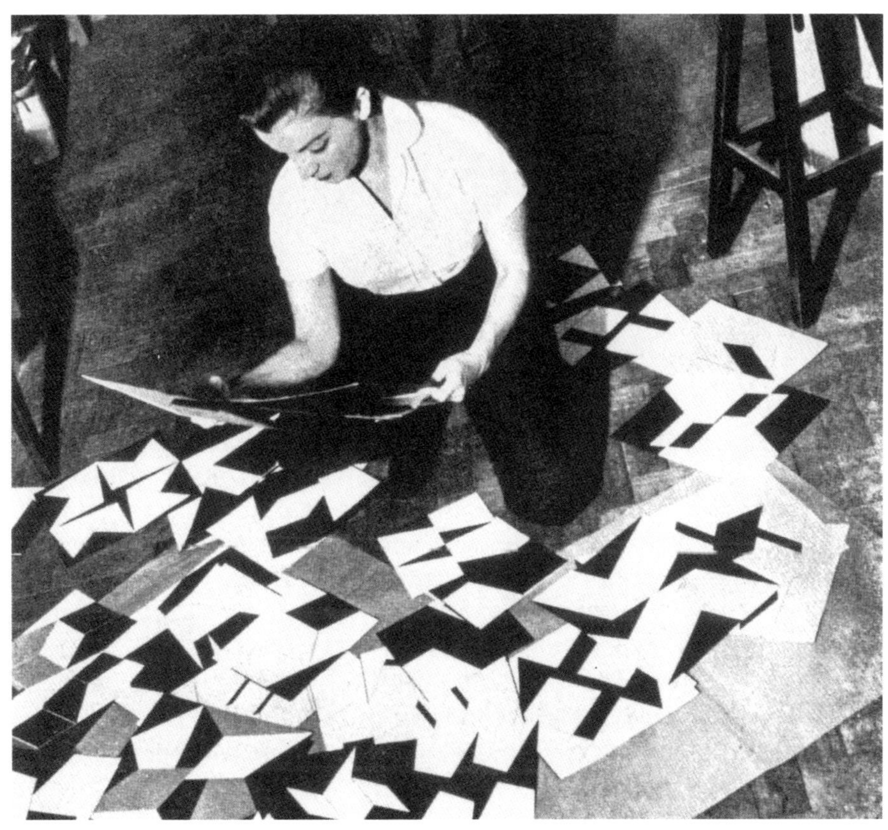

Lygia Clark at her studio
courtesy Associação Cultural O Mundo de Lygia Clark

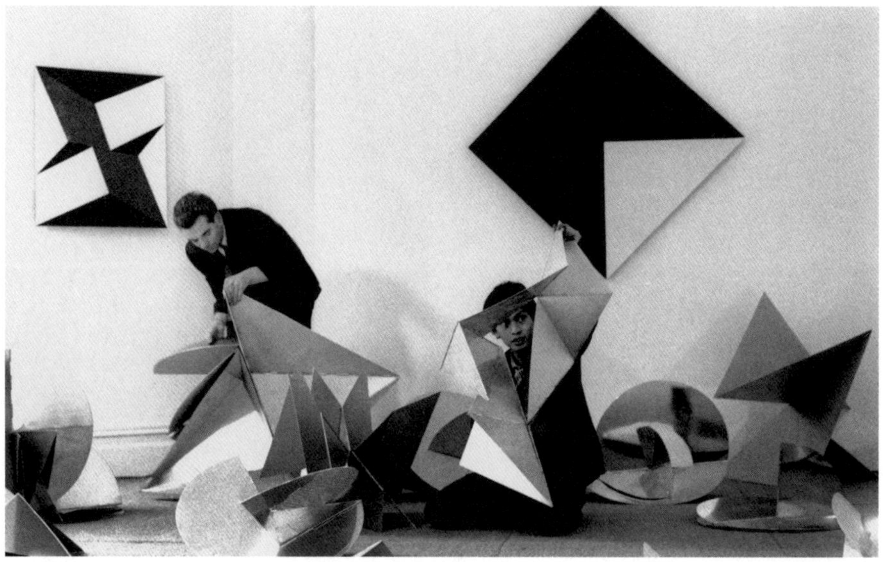

Jornal do Brasil on the eve of the inauguration of the utopian new federal capital Brasilia in 1960. The manifesto's tone was first and foremost reactive to concrete art and poetry while also seeking to 'correct' what its author, Ferreira Gullar, saw as the shortcomings of European Modernism, proposing a 'reinterpretation of neo-plasticism, constructivism and similar movements'.[5] The manifesto was followed in quick succession by an article in which Gullar, upon observing a work by Clark, perceived the increasing ambivalence between the fields of painting and sculpture.[6] Describing that particular artwork as a non-object, Gullar foresaw similar remarks that would emerge years later in the USA, such as those by Donald Judd in the essay 'Specific Objects' and in Dick Higgins' 'Intermedia', regarding minimalism and Fluxus/Conceptual art respectively.[7]

With the increasing international recognition of participatory art and the pioneering practices of former Neoconcrete artists such as Clark, Hélio Oiticica and Lygia Pape, Gullar would later argue that spectator participation emerged out of poetry, from his own use of the page as a means of instigating surprise, of breaking the gradual accretion or subtraction of letters and words typical of concrete

↑ Paul Keeler and David Medalla installing Lygia Clark's sculptures at Signals, London), 1965
photograph by Clay Perry, courtesy England & Co Gallery, London

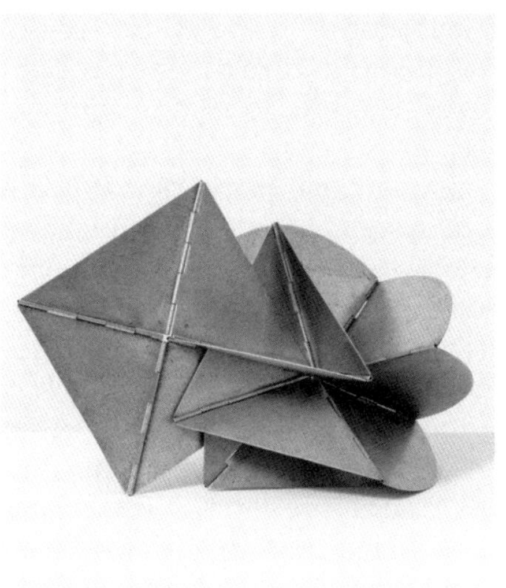 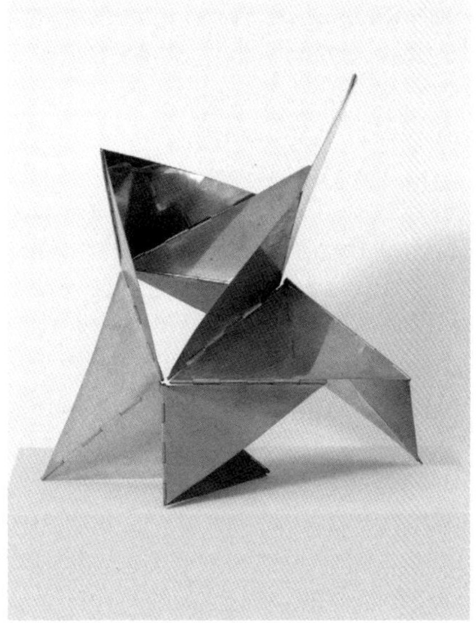

poetry.[8] Self-congratulatory remarks aside, Gullar's observations do nevertheless emphasise the increasing transdisciplinary tendency across cultural production, a tendency that would intensify over the course of the 1960s.

Viewed in retrospect, Lygia Clark's transition from using materials still associated with sculpture per se, to her incorporation of ephemeral, repurposed, discardable day-to-day objects such as plastic bags, elastic bands, ordinary stones, seashells and so forth, may seem coherent with the notion of 'dematerialisation' of the art object as famously celebrated by Lucy Lippard.[9] Yet, the manner through which Clark arrived at such a juncture could not have been more distinct. Arising from the intersecting fields of modern art, architecture and design, Clark's work moved towards kineticism and beyond, incorporating interaction and participation in ways that profoundly challenged presumed relationships between the art object and its beholder.

Clark, at different times and in multiple ways, embraced the topographical figure of the mobius strip. *Caminhando* (Walking) (1963), is an instruction-based action in which the participant is invited to cut along the single-sided surface of a paper mobius strip. As the scissors cut along, inside becomes outside and vice versa, until the original point of incision is reached and surpassed.[10] *Caminhando* refers to that iconic form while transforming it into a formless tangle. Both homage and derision, the action betrays the artist's own productive ambivalence towards the history of art.

In reference to Brazilian art of the post-war era, the mobius strip is a recurrent and undisputed invocation of Max Bill. An artist, designer and former Bauhaus student, Bill was perhaps the most fervent believer in the need for an underlying mathematical basis in artistic creation in accordance with the premises of Theo van Doesburg's 1930 concept of *Art Concret*. Bill had won the international sculpture prize at the first edition of the Bienal de São Paulo in 1951, with a mobius-like aluminium structure entitled *Tripartite Unity* (1951). The award served to further fuel the convictions of a young group of abstract geometrical artists, provoking a whirlwind of enthusiasm and an increasing intransigence across the different local factions, including that of Clark and her interlocutors.

Clark's notion of the 'Organic Line' emerged within her own vocabulary as early as 1954, in describing the interstice between two planes on the surface of her geometric paintings.[11] That notion could be seen to have taken a new turn in 1960 with Clark's *Bichos* (Critters) series, in which configurations of aluminium plates in different simple geometric forms, assembled with hinges, allowed the observer to intervene, articulating them, changing their form according to their own will, or to the structure's own will as the artist herself claimed.[12] Naming those objects *Bichos*, and the consequential 'organic' attributions that Clark made in describing their 'behaviour', admittedly contradicted the premise of 'non-objecthood' defended by Gullar, who still considered the Neoconcrete object as a 'phenomenological pure apparition', in line with van Doesburg's original formulation as an object with no relation to already existing things in the world.[13]

Clark's subsequent interest in psychoanalysis and the therapeutic methods she developed through relational objects arguably led her beyond the disciplinary limits of art itself. The sources for such interests may have preceded the advent of Neoconcretism and therefore problematise strictly formalist interpretations of Clark's creative trajectory.

The transdisciplinary tendencies that would flourish in the mid-1960s may have their roots much earlier. Almir Mavignier, together with Dr Nise da Silveira, founded art workshops at the Pedro II psychi-

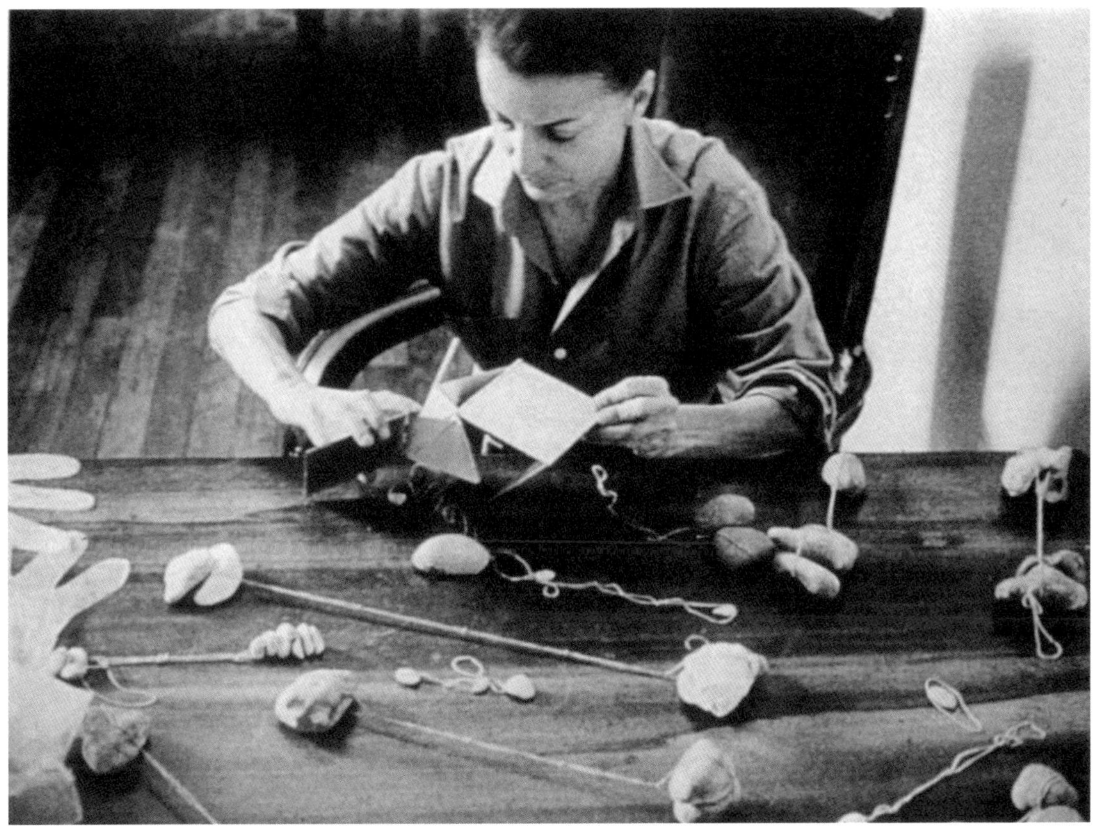

Lygia Clark, *Natureza – Estrutura Cega* (Nature – Blind Structure), 1968
photograph by Michel Desjardins, courtesy Associação Cultural O Mundo de Lygia Clark

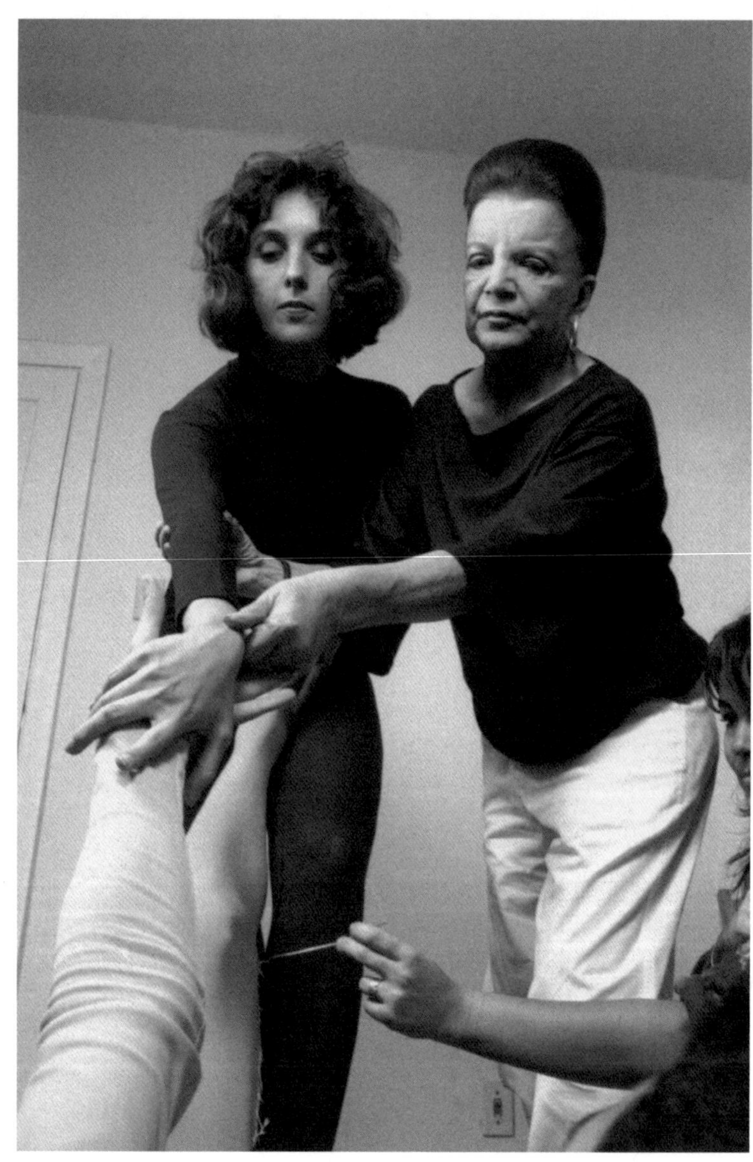

Lygia Clark, *Corpo Coletivo* (Collective Body), Rio de Janeiro, 1984
photograph by Sergio Zalis, courtesy Associação Cultural O Mundo de Lygia Clark

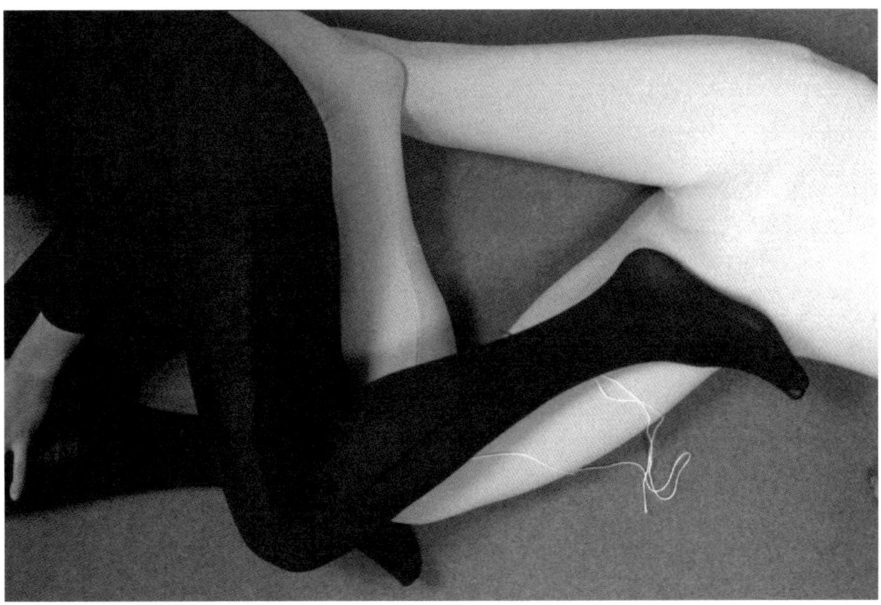

atric hospital in 1947 at the Engenho de Dentro neighbourhood in Rio, inviting artists Ivan Serpa and Abraham Palatnik, and art critic Mário Pedrosa to join them in observing the work of the patients.[14] Such experience had an unquestionable impact on the emerging field of abstract geometrical art in Rio during the 50s, not least in asserting a productive scepticism towards excessive rationalist claims made on behalf of art.

When Clark returned to Brazil after her studies in Paris with Léger, Mavignier had already left Rio to join Max Bill and Tomás Maldonado at the Bauhaus-inspired School of Design at Ulm, in Germany. Serpa had recently won the prize for best young painter, alongside Bill's award for sculpture, at the first edition of the Bienal de São Paulo in 1951. Palatnik, on that same occasion, received an 'honourable mention' since the jury had no idea in which category to place his mechanical-electrical contraption. Today, Palatnik's *Kinechromatic Apparatus* (1951) is rightly recognised as an early and arguably singular example of kinetic art in Brazil, albeit not so much the pioneering intermedia object and event that it undoubtedly was.[15] Pedrosa's intellectual presence and

↑ Lygia Clark, *Corpo Coletivo* (Collective Body), Rio de Janeiro, 1984
photograph by Sergio Zalis, courtesy Associação Cultural O Mundo de Lygia Clark

mentorship, following his thesis on the affective nature of art, served to further consolidate the creative and intellectual environment offered by Serpa's art classes that would lead to the emergence of Grupo Frente around Rio's recently inaugurated Museum of Modern Art.[16] For Clark, such transdisciplinary precedents also relativise the significance of a narrative that focuses strictly upon her formal progression, the breaking of the picture frame, the move towards three-dimensional space and so forth.

With the benefit of hindsight, Lygia Clark is now recognised as a precursor, a pioneer. Increasingly since the 2000s and the rise of so-called 'relational aesthetics' as propagated by Nicolas Bourriaud, or the historicisation of participatory art by scholars such as Claire Bishop, the international relevance of Clark's work has been widely accepted. Similarly, it is no longer sufficient to contextualise Clark's work as evidence of the advances achieved by Brazilian modern and contemporary art as judged through a national post-colonial perspective. Instead, like a strip that alternates between its inside and outside surfaces, the present exhibition approaches that period of art history as it is reflected in the light of the here and now. As such, it is useful to think about the impact of Lygia Clark's work upon subsequent generations of artists beyond Brazil or Latin America by tracing intersecting histories. Indeed, transcultural trajectories often share a common ground, a political and theoretical territory conquered through extraordinary struggles. In the UK such historiographical cross-pollination can be summoned through the work of art critics such as Guy Brett, artists and cultural agitators such as David Medalla and Rasheed Araeen and thinkers such as Stuart Hall and Jean Fisher. Hall exemplified one such transnational correspondence when he invoked the Brazilian experience while discussing the different generations of black and Afro-Caribbean artists in the UK:

> There are many parallels elsewhere with this complex attitude from below to the idea of 'the modern'. There were, of course, the vigorous indigenous modern art movements of India, Africa and Latin America – like the astonishingly bold and formally revolutionary space opened up by Brazilian artists such as Hélio Oiticica and Lygia Clark – since largely written out of the history of Modernism with a capital 'M'.[17]

85

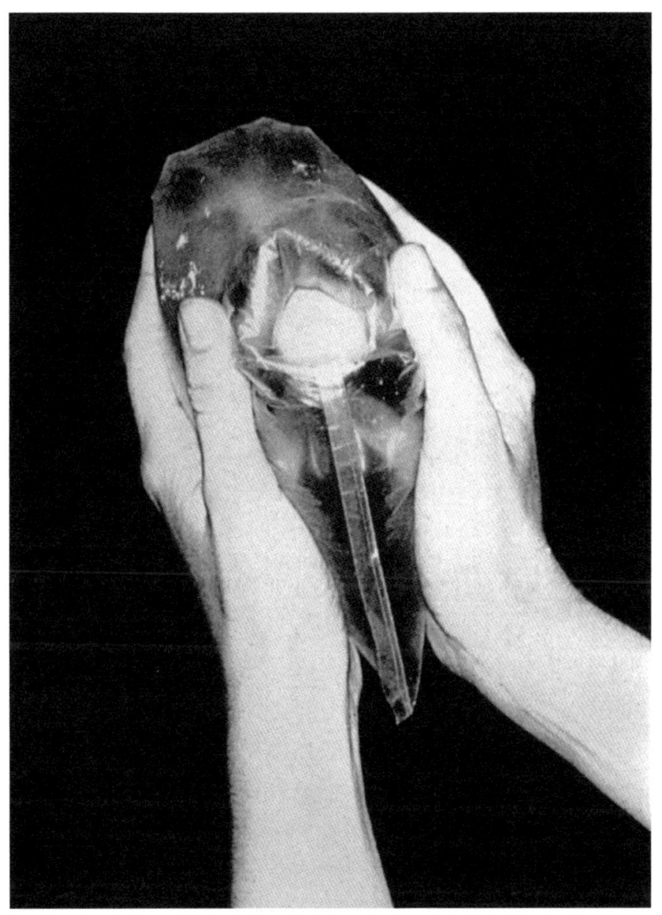

Lygia Clark, *Pedra e Ar* (Stone and Air), 1966
photograph by Vicente de Mello, courtesy Associação Cultural O Mundo de Lygia Clark

It would be hard to uphold such a claim today, given the broad, albeit belated, historical recognition that artists such as Lygia Clark and Hélio Oiticica have since received. Neither did these artists experience – not in their own country at least – what Kobena Mercer has called the 'burden of representation'.[18] Nevertheless, the tortuous route through which they finally attained international recognition – too long a digression to pursue here – brought them into close relation with different generations of artists experiencing what Eddie Chambers described as 'the terrible burden of invisibility and eradication'.[19] Similarly, Jean Fisher identified the source of such a problem as stemming from 'the malodorous trace of this privileged Western canon' when recalling the decade-long struggle that Rasheed Araeen undertook before being 'permitted' to hold the exhibition 'The Other Story: Afro-Asian Artists in Post-war Britain' in 1989–90.[20]

When Hall considered the different attitudes among artists of Afro-Caribbean descent living in the UK, he rightly referred to Clark and Oiticica as being comparable to those from the Windrush generation whereby 'the promise of decolonization liberated them from any lingering sense of inferiority. Their aim was to engage the modern world as equals on its own terrain. [...] They regarded the artistic vocation as a universal calling [...] They claimed art in the name of humanity in general.'[19] How distinct the outlook would be for a generation born in Britain of immigrant parents whose coming of age in the 1980s Hall described as:

> The experience of racialized exclusion bore down in a particular way, subjectively as well as politically, on this second generation. Separated from their homes of origin, marginalized from society's mainstream, excluded and stereotyped, discriminated against in the public sphere, pushed around by the police, abused in the streets, and profoundly alienated from recognition or acceptance by British society at large, they were haunted by questions of identity and belonging. 'Who are we?' 'Where do we come from?' 'Where do we really belong?' Of course, the identity question had already surfaced in the 1970s, and was regarded at the time as not alternative but integral to the politics of black resistance.[22]

Such positionality tran-
spires in much of the work
of the Blk Art Group that
emerged in the West Mid-
lands over the course of
the 1980s. One of the key
artists associated with the
group was Sonia Boyce,
whose early work can be
understood, in an often
nuanced manner, as re-
sponding to the general
conditions that affected
her generation and the
ambivalence of cultural
belonging as described
above by Hall.

In *Big Woman's Talk*
(1984), an intricate pastel
drawing, Boyce captures
a day-to-day scene in
which a curious daugh-
ter, feigning disinterest
through a deceitful day-
dreaming posture, allows herself access to her mother's 'adult' world.
At first sight we may think of the scene as a mere childhood recol-
lection. The detailed living room paraphernalia, the comfy chair, the
mother's floral dress, the decorative wallpaper in the background, are
all suggestive of domestic intimacy. Yet, as we may suspect, such a
reading is insufficient, and the adoption of the image for the promo-
tional poster for 'The Other Story: Afro-Asian Artists in Post-war Britain'
certainly suggests so.

Similarly, Boyce's *She Ain't Holding Them Up, She's Holding On*
(1986) shows the artist holding 'onto' a family portrait with her parents
together with herself and her sister as children. The image is given an
overall coherence through the intricate pattern of a wallpaper that
rushes to the foreground bonding the composition together. This
pastel-on-paper work invokes the intergenerational struggles and
the questions of cultural belonging that arise therein. It featured in the

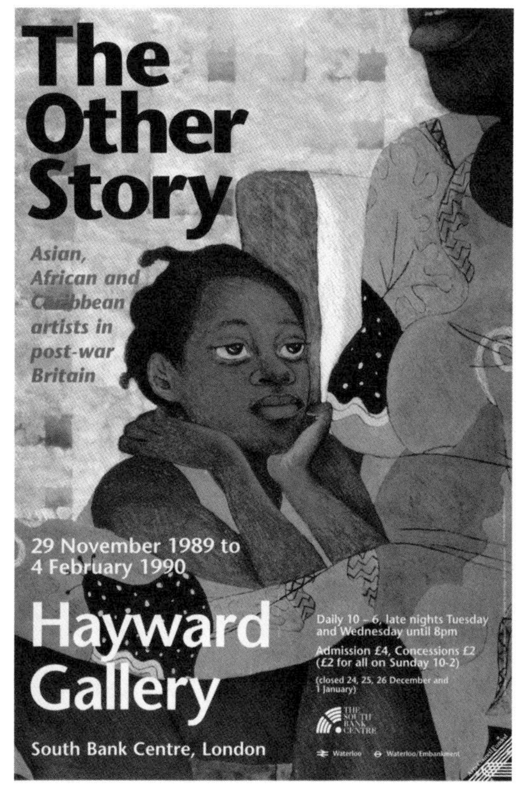

↑ Exhibition poster, 'The Other Story: Asian, African and Caribbean
artists in post-war Britain', 1989, courtesy Hayward Gallery

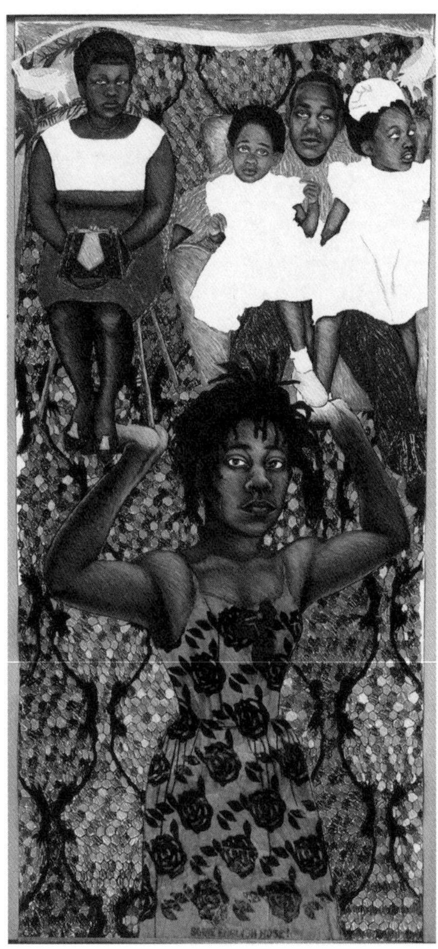

Whitechapel Gallery centenary publication, in reference to the 'From Two Worlds' exhibition for which Boyce also acted as one of the curators. In the caption Boyce stated that: 'I'm talking about the stories and tales that our parents brought with them when they came from the Caribbean'.[23] In the context of Hall's comments above, one would assume that the 'holding on' could also refer, among other things, to the dignity of producing 'art in the name of humanity in general'.

An intergenerational dialogue of a different sort transpired in the first issue of the art journal *Third Text*, another incredibly significant venture initiated by Araeen. In that issue, reverberations from a conversation between John Roberts and Sonia Boyce appeared in an article in which the art critic Guy Brett explored 'the borderline between art life' in the work of Lygia Clark.[24] The article was written in the run-up to Brett curating a section of the exhibition 'Art in Latin America', Dawn Ades' survey of art from the continent, which took place at the Hayward Gallery, London, only a few months prior to Araeen's 'The Other Story', for which Brett and David Medalla also contributed catalogue essays.[25]

In that article, Brett sought to articulate the radicality of a practice that had taken art to its limits and beyond. Viewed in retrospect, and unrelated to Clark's own journey, Boyce undertook a radical leap of her own. From her work with pastels and the representation of domestic scenes with references to family memory, Boyce broadened her practice to include the spontaneous and improvised actions of others,

↑ Sonia Boyce, *Ain't Holding Them Up, She's Holding On* (Some English Rose), 1986
pastels and mixed media on paper, 113.5 x 227 cm
courtesy MIMA – Middlesbrough Institute of Modern Art/DACS

in transdisciplinary means of production as well as display. From the nuanced interrelation between intimacy, identity and wider societal commentary through images charged with subjective and cultural specificity, the artist increasingly invited the subjectivity of the other to interact with the scene, to create the work.

Boyce's *Do You Want to Touch?* (1993) still sustains that interpretative ambivalence between the innocent invitation to gaze, or in this case touch, and the provocative challenge to the other, the onlooker, the gallery visitor. Rather than through the detailed figuration seen in *She Ain't Holding Them Up, She's Holding On*, such ambivalence is now achieved by tactile or haptic means, exploring the possibilities of a culturally charged substance which the artist offers for manipulation: human hair. In writing about *Do You Want to Touch?*, Ian Baucom approaches the subject from the perspective of the absent bodies that the work invokes. He emphasises the interpretative possibilities according to the assumed identity of the addressee in the invitation that constitutes the work's title. On the one hand, as Boyce herself suggested, 'competing signifiers of a polysemous syntax of blackness'. On the other hand, associations regarding racial difference, exoticisation, forms of bias and dominant gazes.[26] Not so much a ready-made but, rather, a kind of relationality charged with fetishism, these scalps, as Baucom put it, relate to the self through, and only because of, the absence of the other. They do not fill a psychological void as in Clark's use of relational objects in her *Estruturação do Self* therapy propositions, but it is precisely because of the void that they inherently carry – the absence of the other – that touch is permitted, that the relation is allowed by Boyce's invitation, as intrusive as that might feel.

Boyce remembered Clark's pioneering workshops with students at the Sorbonne when proposing an improvised action at Villa Arson in Nice with students being 'animated' by dancer-choreographer Vânia Gala and grunge rapper Astronautalis. Yet a crucial difference separates the work of Clark and Boyce. The act of inviting the other to participate is not sufficient in establishing a direct relation, a genealogical connection.

In presenting her own participatory events to gallery audiences, Boyce returns to the device of the wallpaper, only now reconfigured, *wrapping* the diverse video documentation of performances together. In her pastels on paper Boyce had made use of the wallpaper as a flattening device for the picture, merging the often-geometrical patterns of the background with the picture's central protagonists. Such was the case in *Missionary Position I* and *II* (1985), where the geometrical patterns of the wallpaper feature so prominently in the foreground. Boyce plays here with the ambivalence of the scene. The wallpaper brings together the sexual innuendo of the title and the critical action being depicted.

A reversal of sorts therefore may be observed. Today, Boyce's wallpaper has transcended the two-dimensional, illusionary space of the picture to occupy real space. In *Lover's Rock*, (1998), *Devotional* (ongoing since 1999) and *We move in her way* (2017), wallpaper acts upon the gallery space, establishing or perhaps recovering a recognisable pattern, an identity, drawn from the recorded improvised action.

If Clark, in the most formal of all descriptions of her work, broke away from the picture plane to bring her 'organic' geometry into space, Boyce's project seems to be entirely other: not quite recovering a trace from the live performance, but as reconfigured mementos, geometricised through a process of mirroring, or as stylised figures in the graphic manner of safety instruction manuals. More importantly, in this process of reconfiguration, Boyce demonstrates that, unlike Clark, she is not willing to entirely let go, to give up her control.

In translating those 'moving scenes' into 'wallpaper' configurations, it is as if Boyce intends to 'ground' the loose, participatory, intuitive and improvised action within the space, to give it a sense of permanence, of belonging. There is absolutely no intention to abandon art here, to allow the other to 'violate' the artist as Clark once bluntly put it, but instead, one notes a clear quest to 'be-with' the performance and by extension the participant.[27] Writing about Boyce's work, Fisher stated that:

> Being is in essence 'being-with'. And being-with, for the human infant, is first experienced through touch and hearing: the rhythmic and arhythmic sounds of the maternal body and, later, the voice of the other without which the human does not learn to speak. The 'other' is always internal to the self.[28]

Fisher's words could quite easily be applied to Clark's work, to the series *Nostalgia do Corpo* (Nostalgia for the Body), produced between

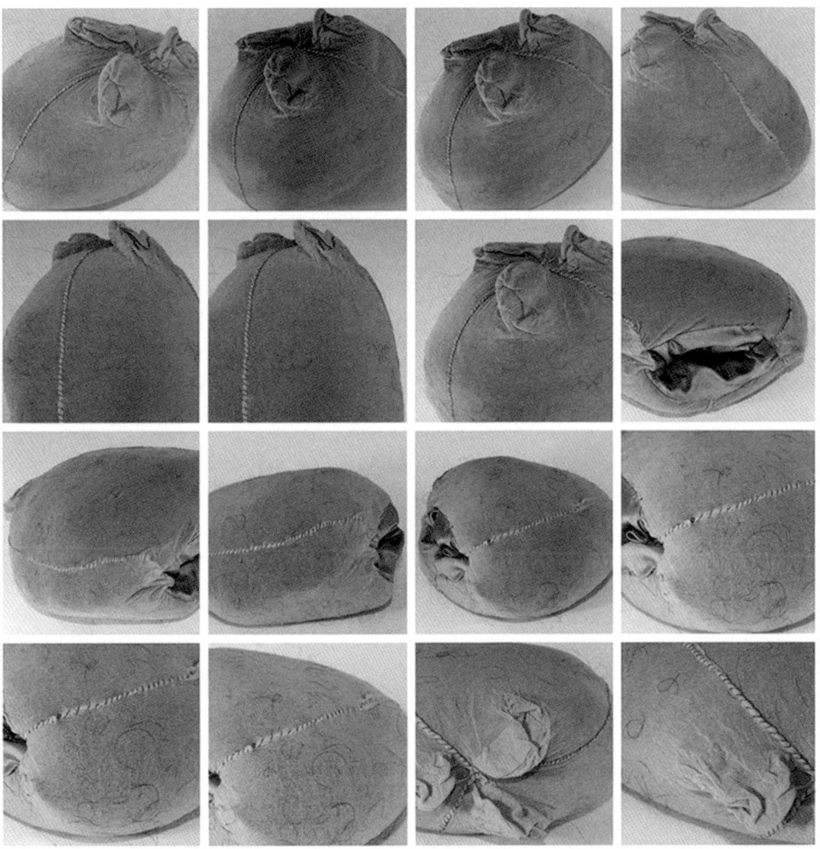

↑ Sonia Boyce, *Three Pairs of Tights Stuffed with Afro Hair*, 2015
photographic print on dibond, 80 x 80 cm

1966 and 1968 which involve elastic bands, plastic bags and other simple materials through which participants interact.

Exiled in 1969, Caetano Veloso composed 'If You Hold a Stone' (1971) in homage to Lygia Clark's *Pedra e Ar* (Stone and Air) (1966). Like the intersubjective play in *The I and the You*, the song reveals as much about the psychological state of its author as it describes his wonder and astonishment at experiencing Clark's simple proposition. The work itself consists of a stone placed on top of a plastic bag filled with air, which is held between one's palms. The stone thus oscillates, up and down, according to the pressure one applies to the bag.

From London, Veloso wrote his lyrics in English with the exception of the refrain, which is not only in Portuguese but also reproduces the well-known chant, 'Marinheiro Só' (The Lone Sailor). Such chants accompany the Afro-Brazilian martial art of Capoeira, inciting or commenting on the action of the 'players', similar to the manner in which antiphony acts within musical improvisation.[29] Capoeira, originally devised by enslaved Afro-descendants as a fight disguised as dance, serves as an apt metaphor for the transmedia practice at play among film-makers, musicians, artists, poets and so many of Veloso's interlocuters at the time, perhaps best encapsulated by Oiticica's own description of his art as 'music'.[30]

'Marinheiro Só' invokes the image of the lone sailor struggling against the environment to reach home, to return to Bahia, the Brazilian state with the strongest Afro-descendent cultural heritage and, as it happens, also Veloso's birthplace. With 'If You Hold a Stone' the singer, who later became one of Clark's 'patients' in her private *Estruturação do Self* (Structuring the Self) therapy sessions, pays homage to both the artist and his own Bahiano identity. The double meaning, so characteristic of Capoeira, is now transfigured to describe his own, and by extension Clark's exiled condition. It is also astonishing how distinct and yet similar observations are drawn by Fisher while discussing Boyce's *For you, only you* (2007):

> Nowadays antiphony, or 'call and response', is more readily associated with the formal structure of black music where, as Paul Gilroy asserts, it carries the potential of nondominating social relationships: 'Lines between self and other are blurred and special forms of pleasure are created as a result of the meetings and conversations that are established

between one fractured, incomplete, and unfinished racial self and others.' As 'meeting and conversation' between one (linguistically) incomplete self and others, antiphony in *For you, only you* speaks both to these hospitable forms of sociality and to the pathos of the diasporic subject, needing to negotiate a sense of belonging between displacement from the place of departure and cultural estrangement from the place of arrival, in which he or she must bear the mark of difference. [31]

Boyce's practice has referenced and archived music as a means of demarcating and/or asserting specific cultural spaces, as in *Devotional Wallpaper and Placards* (2008–2020).

With *Lover's Rock*, Boyce transposes the lyrics of Susan Cadogan's 1975 'Hurt so Good' onto the wall of the gallery space in reference to the memory, whether collective and/or personal, of a social scene, the house parties where the track would have been played in the 1970s. There is something of an unexpected encounter in the coming together of different forms of desire, whether sexual or not. The erotic charge of Cadogan's song would evoke 'the marks against the wall after the dance, the rubbing of the body', as Boyce recalls, fuelling her own desire to bring the work into the space, 'to make the text more physical'.[32] Cadogan's song and Veloso's 'If You Hold a Stone' are brought together here, in the conjunction of two exhibitions. *The I and the You* are thus set together, or against each other, in *An Awkward Relation*.

Michael Asbury

1. The work was recently included by curator Eldina Begic in the exhibition 'Workwear: How to Wear Utopia', Het Nieuwe Instituut, Rotterdam, March–September 2023.

2. Tania Riveira, 'Baba, Falo, Vagina. As Fabulações Queer e Feministas de Lygia Clark', in *Lygia Clark Projeto Para Um Planeta*, eds. Ana Maria Maia & Pollyana Quintella (exh. cat.) (São Paulo: Pinacoteca, 2024) 129–144, 138.

3. Clark, 'Letter to Piet Mondrian', May 1959, translated into English in *Lygia Clark: The Abandonment of Art, 1948-1988*, eds. Cornelia Butler & Luis Pérez-Oramas (exh. cat.) (New York: MoMA, 2014) 59.

4. Interview with Yve-Alain Bois, Suely Rolnik: *Archive pour une œuvre-événement – Projet d'activation de la mémoire corporelle d'une trajectoire artistique et son contexte* [DVD] ed. Suely Rolnik (Paris: Carta Blanca Editions, 2010). A collection of twenty interviews on the subject of Lygia Clark and spectator participation.

5. Ferreira Gullar (and other signatories), 'Manifesto Neoconcreto', originally published in 'Suplemento Dominical', *Jornal do Brasil* (22 March 1959). English translation in *Art in Latin America: The Modern Era 1820–1980*, ed. Dawn Ades (New Haven and London: Yale University Press, 1989) 335.

6. Ferreira Gullar, 'Theory of the Non-Object', Suplemento Dominical, *Jornal do Brasil* (19–20 December, 1959).

7. Several authors have stated such a precedent, including myself, see Michael Asbury, 'Neoconcretism and Minimalism: On Ferreira Gullar's Theory of the Non-Object', in *Cosmopolitan Modernisms*, ed. Kobena Mercer (London: inIVA and Cambridge, MA: The MIT Press, 2005) 168–89. Included in the page range a translation of Gullar's 'Theory of the Non-Object' is provided.

8. A special edition of *Third Text* on Brazilian art, contains two excellent articles on Fereira Gullar and the legacy of Neoconcretism, and an essay on Lygia Clark, see Sergio Bruno Martins, 'Phenomenological Openness', 79-90, Irene Small, 'Exit and Impasse', and Tania Riveira, 'Ethics, Psychoanalysis and Postmodern Art in Brazil', in 'Bursting on the Scene: Looking Back at Brazilian Art', *Third Text*, guest ed. Sérgio Bruno Martins, Number 114, January 2012. 79–90, 91–101, 53–63 On Neoconcretism, see also, Mariola V. Alvarez, *The Affinity of Neoconcretism: Interdisciplinary Collaborations in Brazilian Modernism, 1954–1964* (Berkeley: University of California Press, 2023) 30–70.

9. *Six Years: The Demateri-alization of the Art Object from 1966 to 1972*, ed. Lucy Lippard (New York: Praeger, 1973).

10. The direction one took from that point, to the right or to the left of the original incision, was for Clark the critical point of the action, the crucial decision from where there would be no return. See Manuel J. Borja-Villel et al. (eds.), *Lygia Clark* (exh. cat.), touring retrospective exhibition (Barcelona: Fundació Antoni Tapies, 1997–99) 151.

11. A nuanced distinction exists between Clark's notion of the 'organic line' and the contemporaneous employment of the term 'organicism' by British artists in reference to the work of Scottish biologist and mathematician Darcy Wentworth Thompson. In both cases the use of the term 'organic' stems from the acknowledgement of the mathematical basis underlying all form. However, if for Clark the organic arose out of geometrical formations, among her British contemporaries, as in Thompson's original study, it was geometry that emerged from nature, out of organic formations.

12. *Bichos* have been translated as animals, beasts, critters or creatures. While individually none of these fulfil the precise meaning of the term, collectively they come close to describing the meaning of Bichos in Portuguese.

13. In Gullar's words: "The non-object is not an anti-object but a special object through which a synthesis of sensorial and mental experiences is intended to take place. It is a transparent body in terms of phenomenological knowledge: while being entirely perceptible it leaves no trace. It is a pure appearance." op. cit.

Amongst Theo van Doesburg's tenets of *Art Concret* was: "a painting has no meaning other than itself", see, 'Basis of Concrete painting', in: *Revue Art Concret* (Paris: May 1930).

14. Today housed at the Museu de Imagens do Inconsciente, Rio de Janeiro. For a thorough analysis of the intersection of mental health and the avant-garde in Brazil, see Kaira M. Cabañas, *Learning from Madness: Brazilian Modernism and Global Contemporary Art* (Chicago: University of Chicago Press, 2018).

15. According to the artist, the *Kinechromatic Apparatus* was a direct reaction to his observations of the paintings by patients at Engenho de Dentro, See Michael Asbury, 'Some Notes on Abraham Palatnik's *Kinechromatic Apparatus*', in *Abraham Palatnik: a reinvenção da pintura*, eds. Felipe Scovino & Pieter Tjabbes (exh. cat.) (Brasilia: Centro Cultural Banco do Brasil, 2013) 61–77.

16. For an English translation of much of Pedrosa's art criticism, see *Mário Pedrosa an Anthology*, MoMA Primary Documents series, eds. Glória Ferreira & Paulo Herkenhoff (Durham: Duke University Press, 2015).

17. Stuart Hall, 'Assembling the 1980s: The Deluge – and After', in *Shades of Black*, eds. David A. Bailey, Ian Baucom and Sonia Boyce (Durham, NC: Duke University Press, 2005) 1–20, 6.

18. The expression refers to the unrealistic expectation common in the 1980s, that one should, given the opportunity, represent the entirety of the culture or the diasporic minority to which one belongs. Kobena Mercer, 'Iconography after Identity', in *Shades of Black* (Durham: Duke University Press, 2005) 49–58, 56. This burden is nevertheless sometimes attributed to Oiticica, who through his own writing has often been understood as bringing together the modern Brazilian experience, bridging in other words, Antropofagia with Tropicalia through Neoconcretism. This interpretation becomes all the more problematic when Oiticica is uncritically equated with samba and the black culture of the Favela.

19. Eddie Chambers, *Black Artists in British Art: A History since the 1950s* (London and New York: I.B. Taurus, 2014) 2.

20. Jean Fisher, 'The Other Story and the Past Imperfect', *Tate Papers*, no.12 (Autumn 2009).

21. Hall, op. cit., 5–6.

22. Ibid., 18.

23. *The Whitechapel Art Gallery Centenary Review*, ed. Catherine Lampert et al. (London: Whitechapel Art Gallery, 2001) 116.

24. I am grateful to Gilane Tawadros for bringing this juxtaposition to our attention. See our conversation in this publication 50–71.

25. 'Sonia Boyce in Conversation with John Roberts' and Guy Brett, 'Lygia Clark: The Borderline between Art Life', *Third Text*, vol. 1, issue 1 (Autumn 1987) 55–64 and 65–94.

26. Ian Baucom, 'Every Bit of It. All Complete', in *The Unmapped Body: 3 Black British Artists* (exh. cat.) (New Haven: Yale University Art Gallery, 1998–99). 5–20, 10.

27. See excepts from letters between Clark and Oiticica in Claire Bishop (ed.), *Participation,* Documents of Contemporary Art, (Cambridge, MA: The MIT Press and London: Whitechapel Gallery, 2006) 111.

28. Jean Fisher, 'For you, only you: The Return of the Troubadour', in *Sonia Boyce: Thoughtful Disobedience,* ed. Sophie Orlando (Dijon: Les Presses du Réel and Nice: Villa Arson, 2017). Fisher quotes Paul Gilroy, *The Black Atlantic* (London: Verso, 1993) 42–55, 44.

29. Typical of its syncretic nature, a martial art disguised as dance, the opponents in the 'game' of capoeira are described as 'players'.

30. Hélio Oiticica, 'De Hélio Oiticica para Biscoitos Finos', unpublished document, 11 November, 1979; Projeto Hélio Oiticica: Arquive Doc. n.0057.79, 1–8, 2.

31. Fisher, 'For you, only you: The Return of the Troubadour', op. cit., 78.

32. 'Wallpaper: Sonia Boyce and Christine Woods Interviewed by Andrea Mackean', in *Sonia Boyce: Performance (Annotations 2)*, ed. Mark Crinson (London: InIVA, 1998) 34–39, 35.

Lygia
Clark

Lygia Clark, *Composição*, 1954
alkyd paint on wood, 48.8 x 74.4 cm, coleção Claudio Valansi
© Associação Cultural O Mundo de Lygia Clark

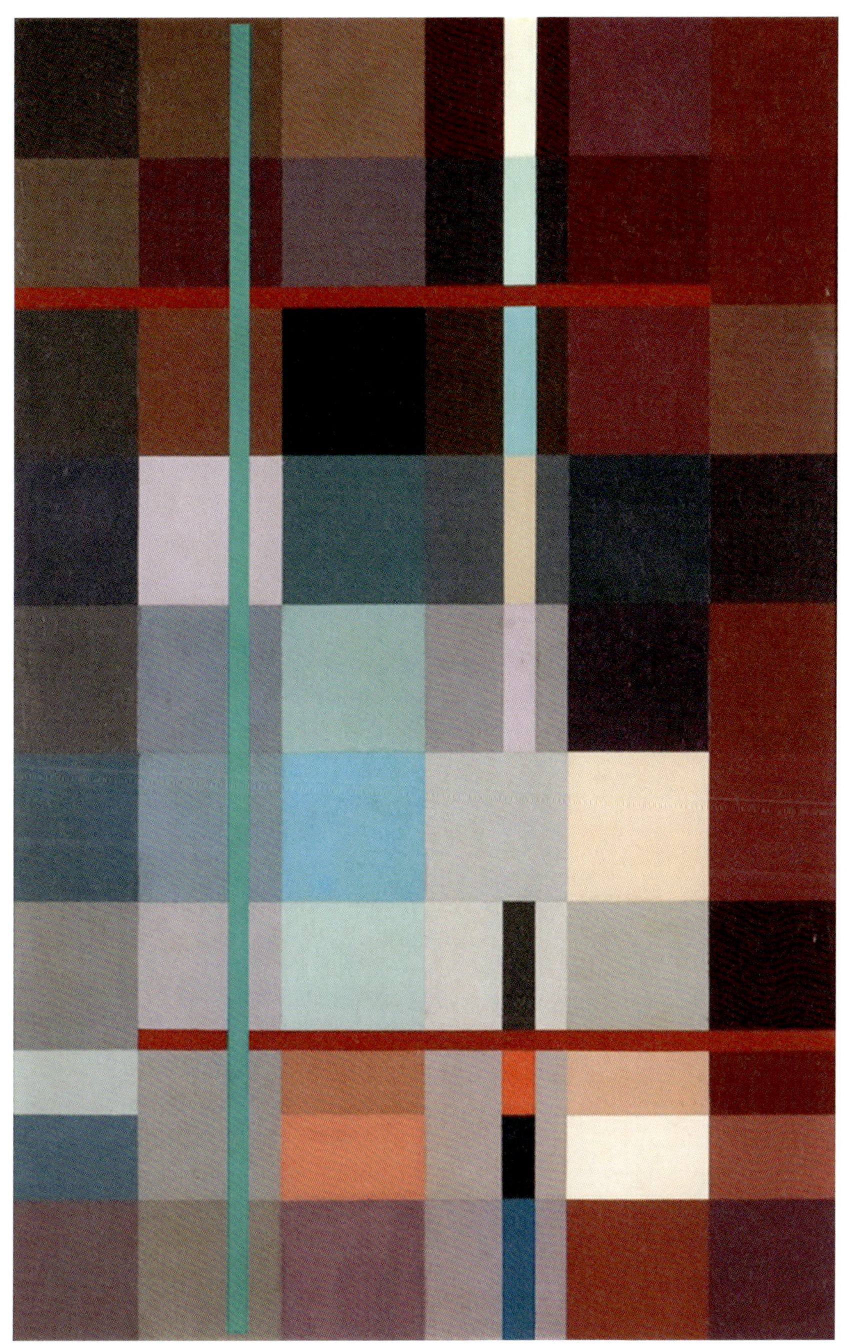

Lygia Clark, *Superfície Modulada* (Modulated surface), 1955
acrylic on eucatex, 65 x 65 cm, coleção Marcos Ribeiro Simon
courtesy Almeida & Dale, São Paulo © Associação Cultural O Mundo de Lygia Clark

100

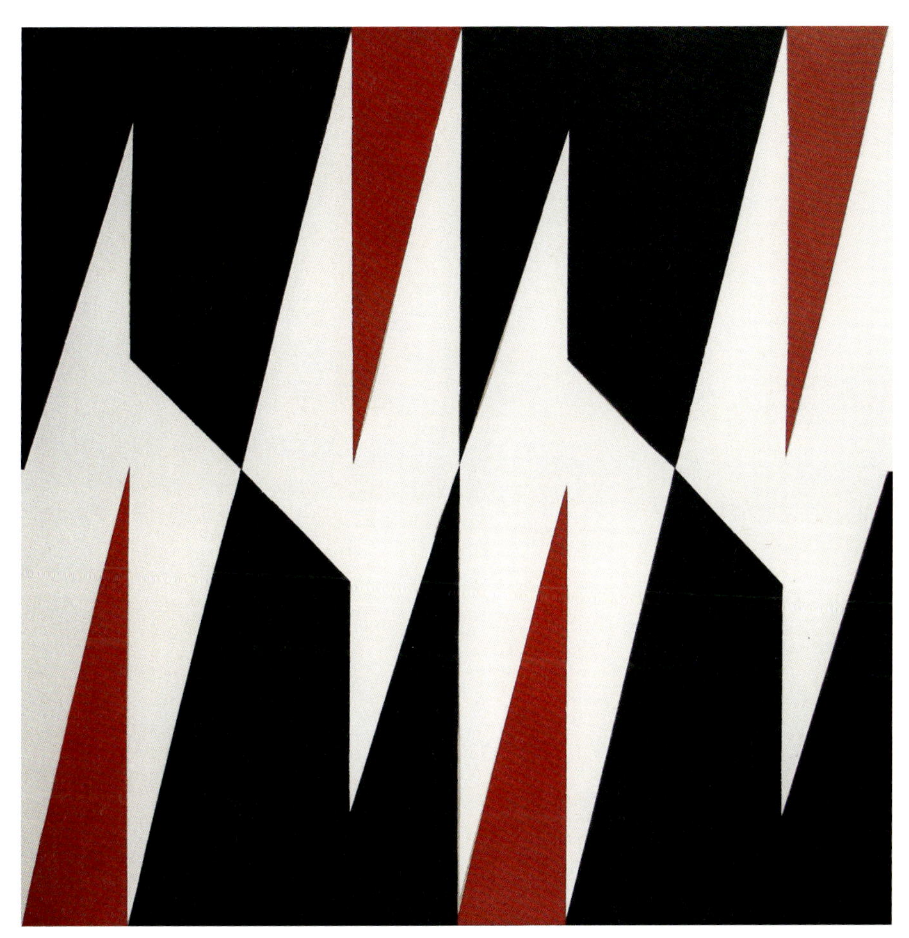

Lygia Clark, *Planos em superfície modulada, serie B, n.7, versão 1*, 1958
automotive paint on chipboard, 100 x 100 cm, Rose and Alfredo Setubal Collection
photograph by Alexandre dos Santos Silva, courtesy Almeida & Dale, São Paulo
© Associação Cultural O Mundo de Lygia Clark

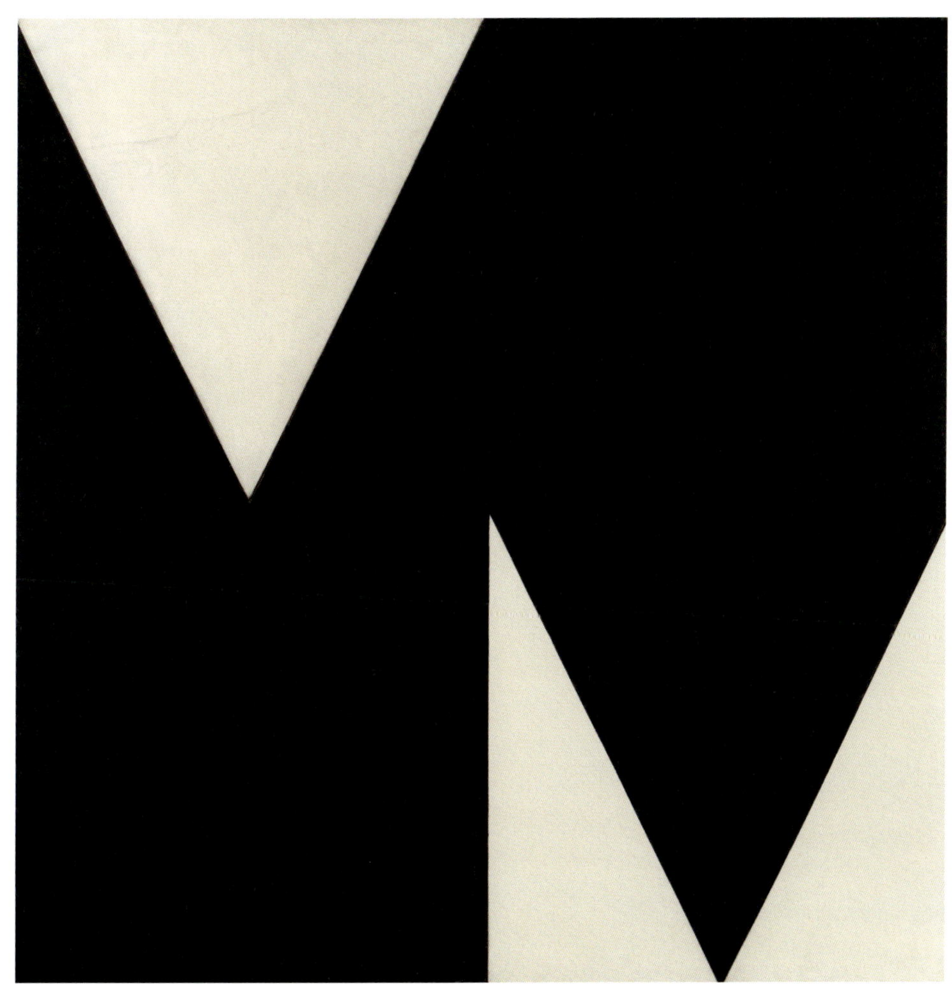

Lygia Clark, *Superficie Modulada*, 1958/1984
industrial ink on wood, 42 x 63 cm, courtesy Estate of Lygia Clark and Alison Jacques, London
© Associação Cultural O Mundo de Lygia Clark.

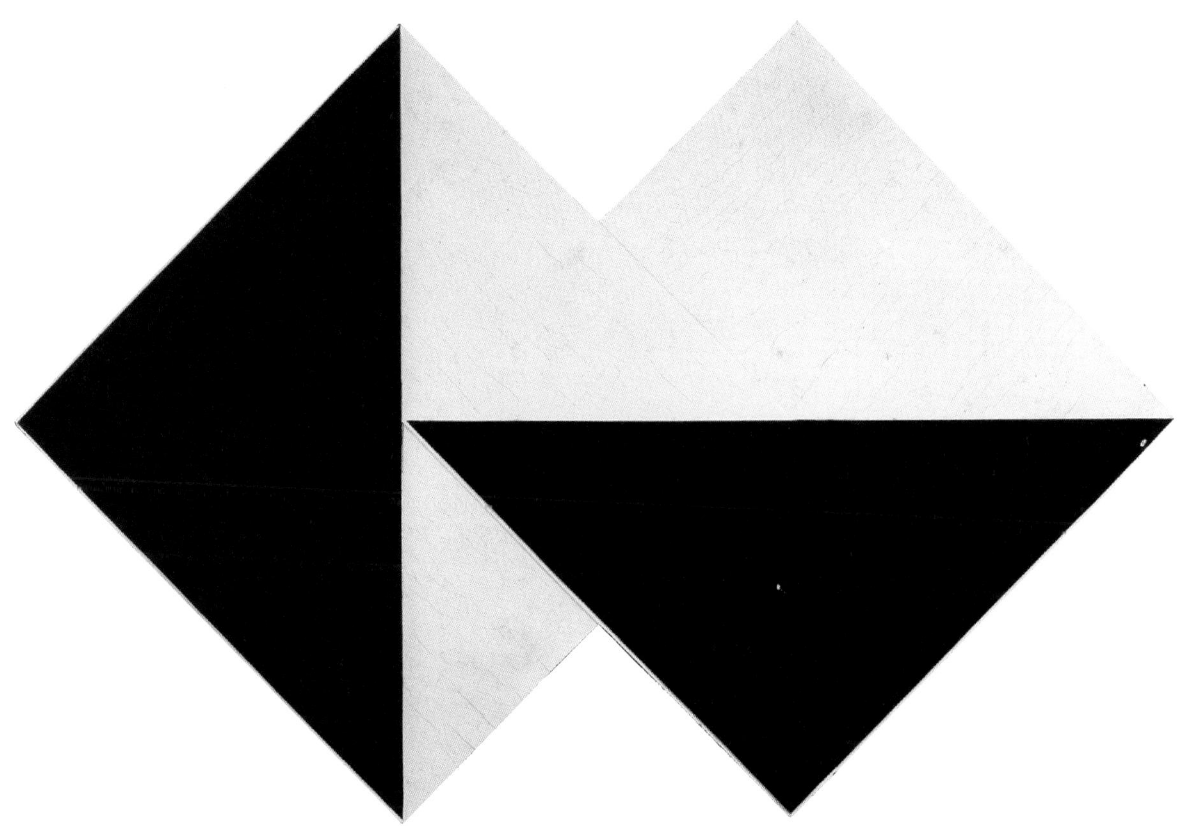

Lygia Clark, *Bicho*, 1960–84
steel, 50 x 45 x 40 cm, courtesy Estate of Lygia Clark and Alison Jacques, London
© Associação Cultural O Mundo de Lygia Clark

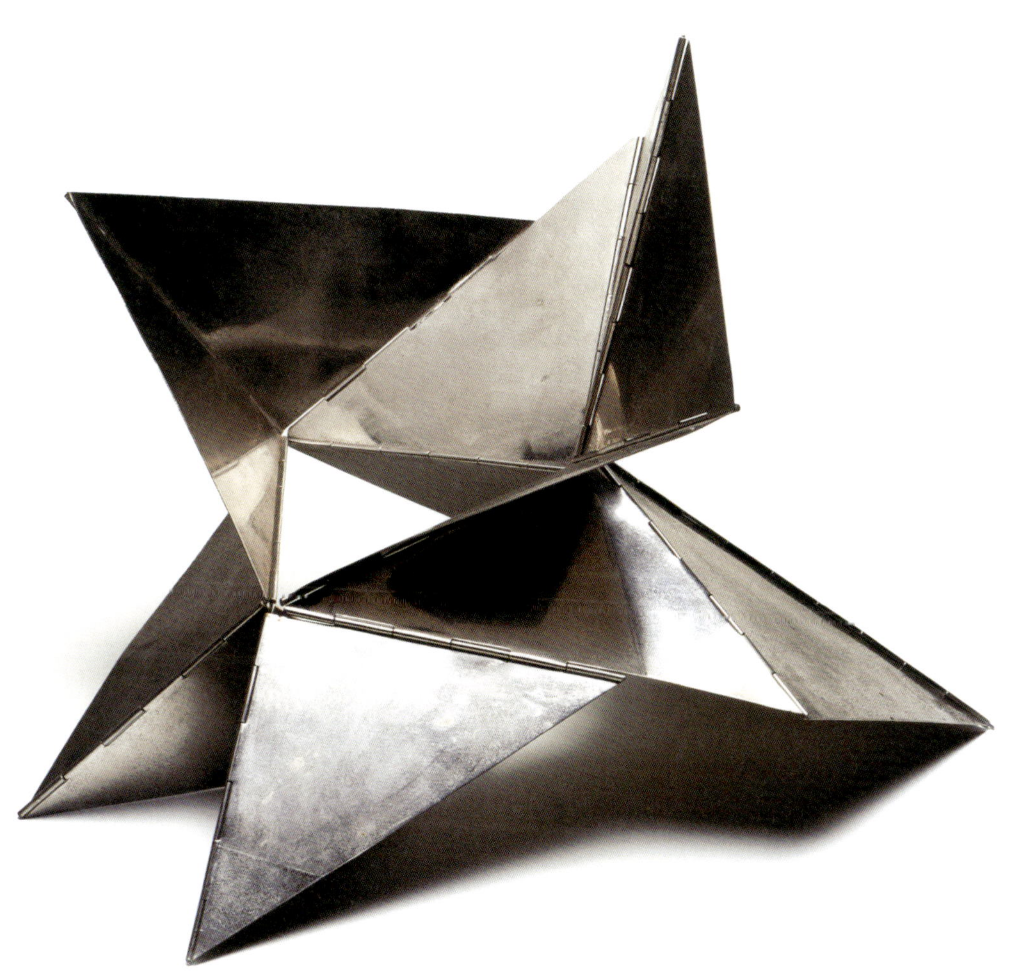

Lygia Clark, *Bicho de Bolso* (Pocket Bicho), 1967
aluminium, 13 x 20 x 10 cm, photograph by Michel Desjardins
courtesy Associação Cultural O Mundo de Lygia Clark

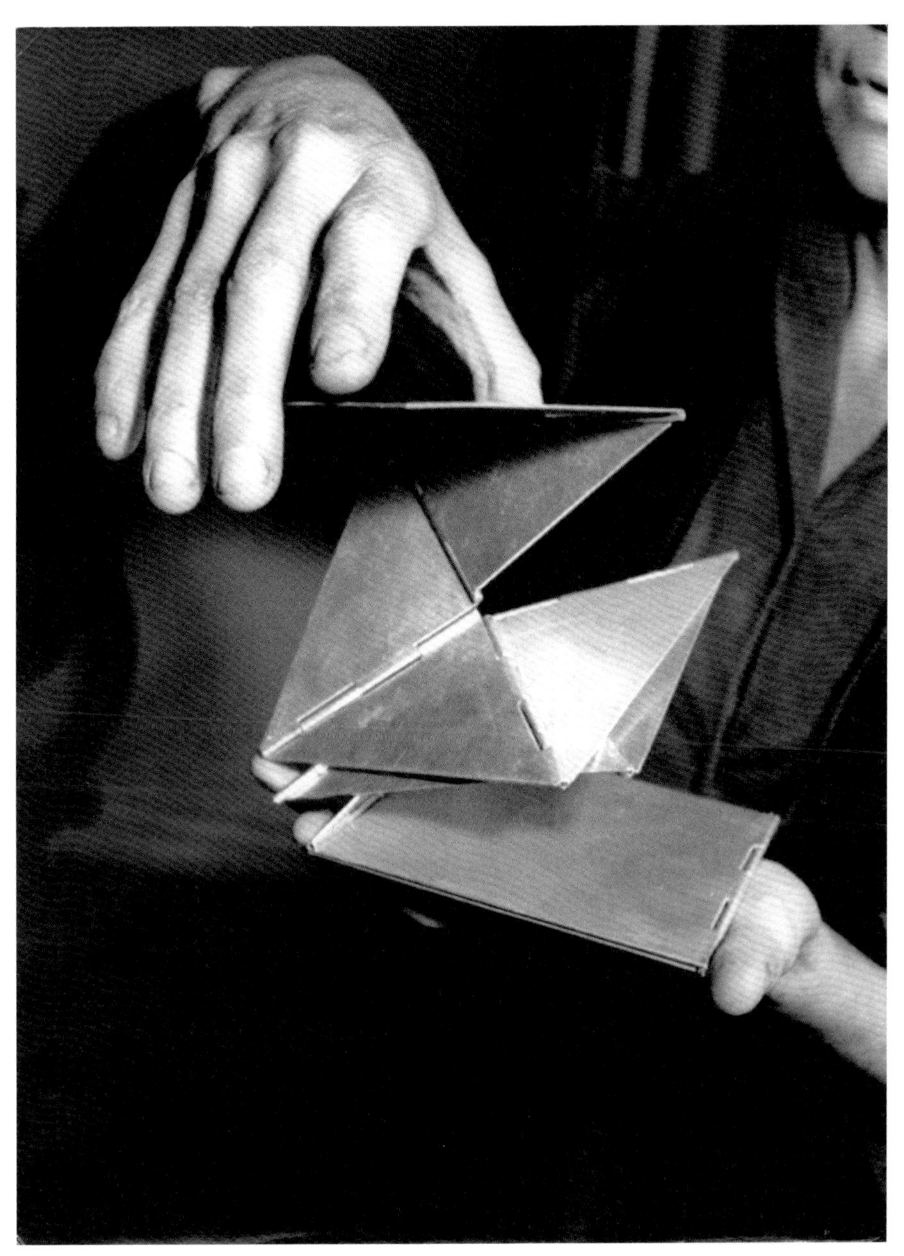

Lygia Clark, *Estruturas de Caixa de Fósforos (Dourado)* ↗
/ Matchbox Structure (Gold), 1964
gouache paint, matchboxes, 7 x 9 x 8 cm
photograph by Michael Brzezinski,
collection of Guy & Alexandra Brett, courtesy Alison Jacques, London
© Associação Cultural O Mundo de Lygia Clark

Lygia Clark, *Estruturas de Caixa de Fósforos (Preto e Branco)* ↘
/ Matchbox Structure (Black and White), 1964
gouache paint, matchboxes, 8.5 x 7 x 5.8 cm
photograph by Michael Brzezinski,
collection of Guy & Alexandra Brett, courtesy Alison Jacques, London
© Associação Cultural O Mundo de Lygia Clark

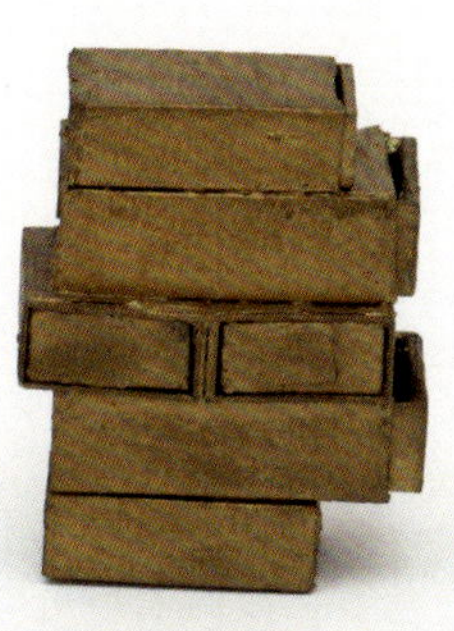

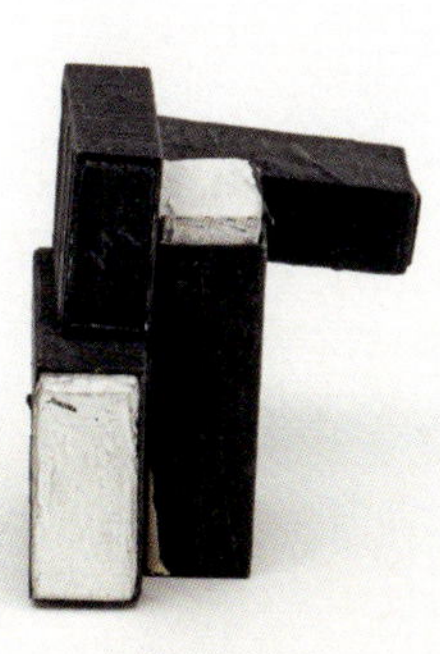

Lygia Clark, *Livro Obra* (Book work), Copy J, 1983
coated paper, cutouts, folding coloured cardboard,
acetate envelopes, graphite and ink, 21.3 x 21.3 x 8 cm, private collection
photograph by Fernanda de Souza Barbosa
courtesy Associação Cultural O Mundo de Lygia Clark

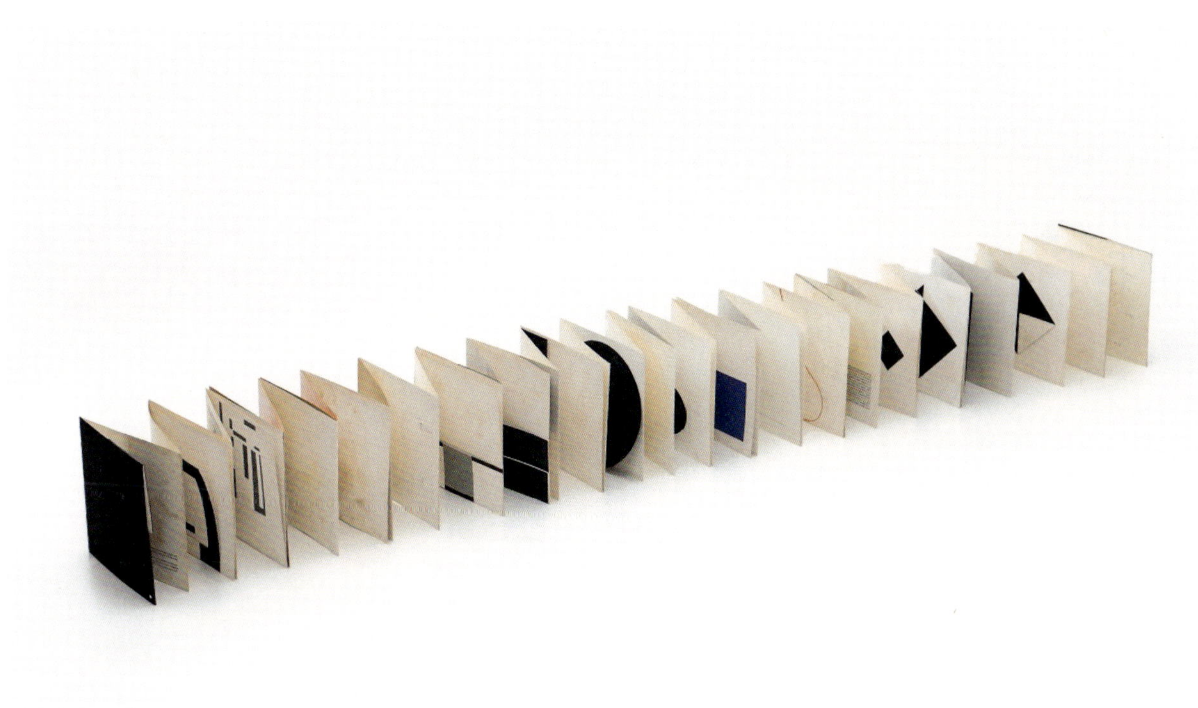

Lygia Clark, *Caminhando* (Walking), 1963
photograph by Virna Santolia, courtesy Associação Cultural
O Mundo de Lygia Clark

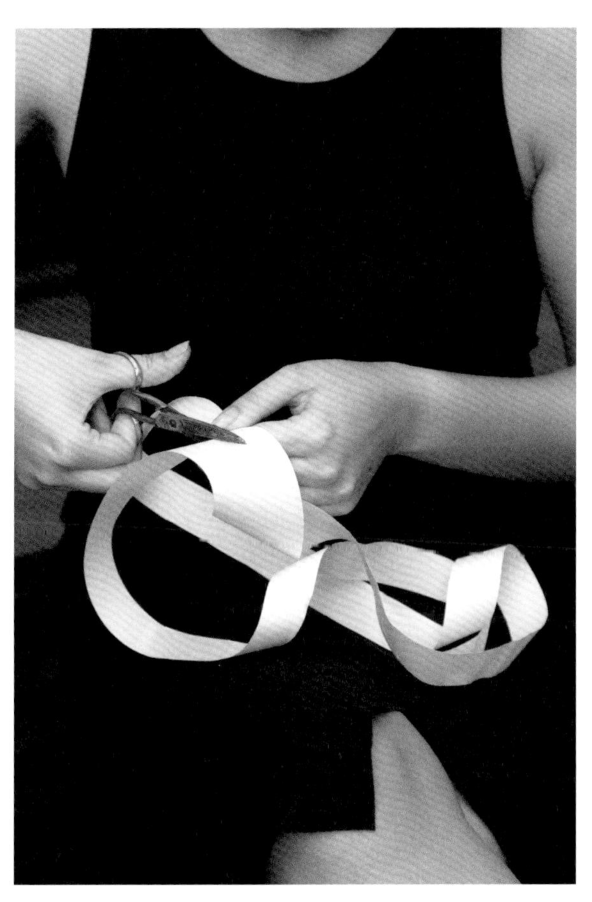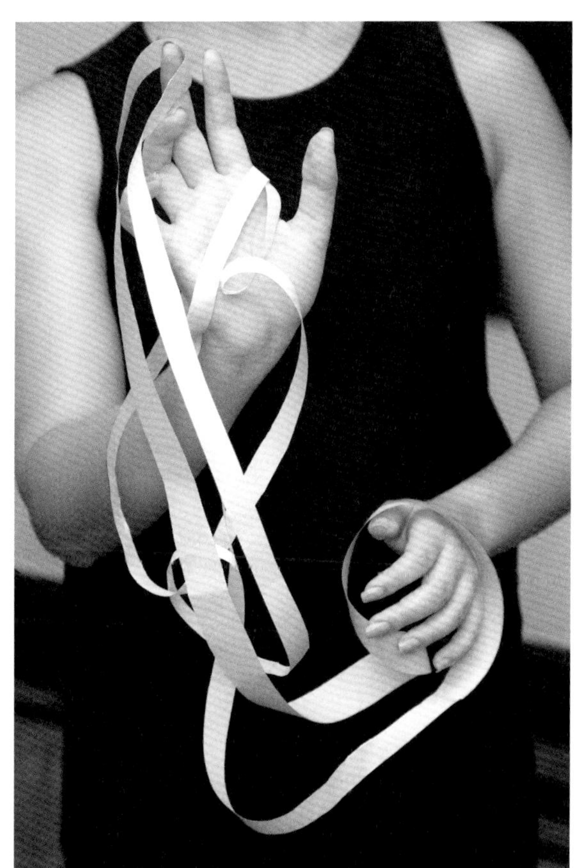

Lygia Clark, *Diálogo de Óculos* (Glasses Dialogue), 1966 ↗
aluminium, rubber and mirrored glass, photograph by Eduardo Clark
courtesy Associação Cultural O Mundo de Lygia Clark

Lygia Clark, *Óculos* (Glasses), 1966 ↘
aluminium, rubber and mirrored glass, photograph by Eduardo Clark
courtesy Associação Cultural O Mundo de Lygia Clark

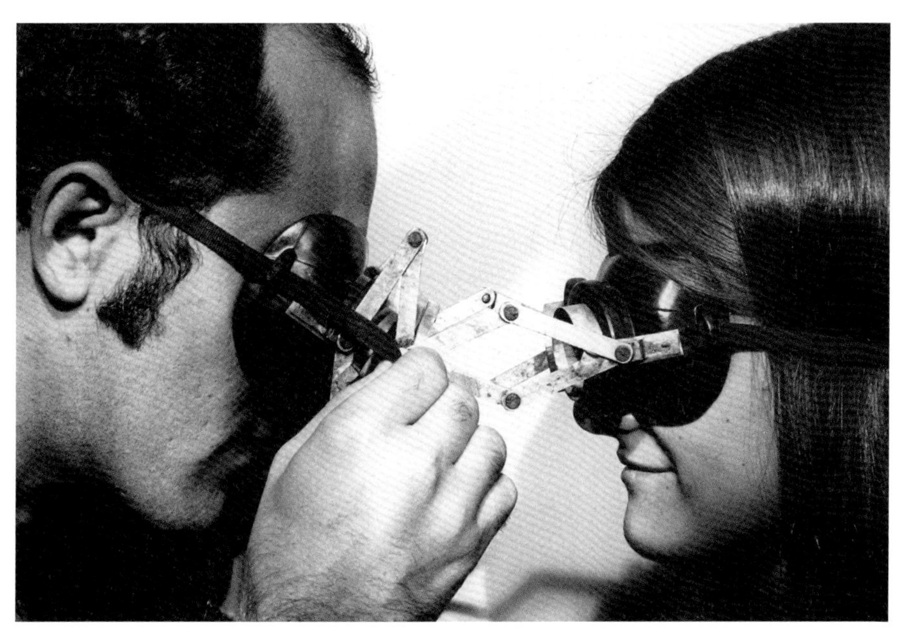

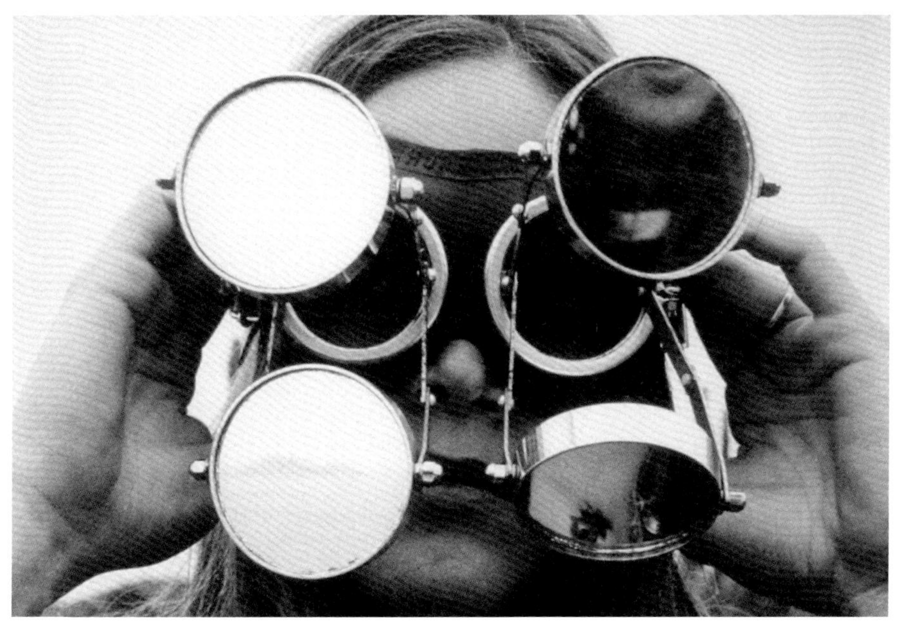

Lygia Clark, *Pedra e Ar* (Stone and air), 1966
photograph by Vicente de Mello, courtesy Associação Cultural
O Mundo de Lygia Clark

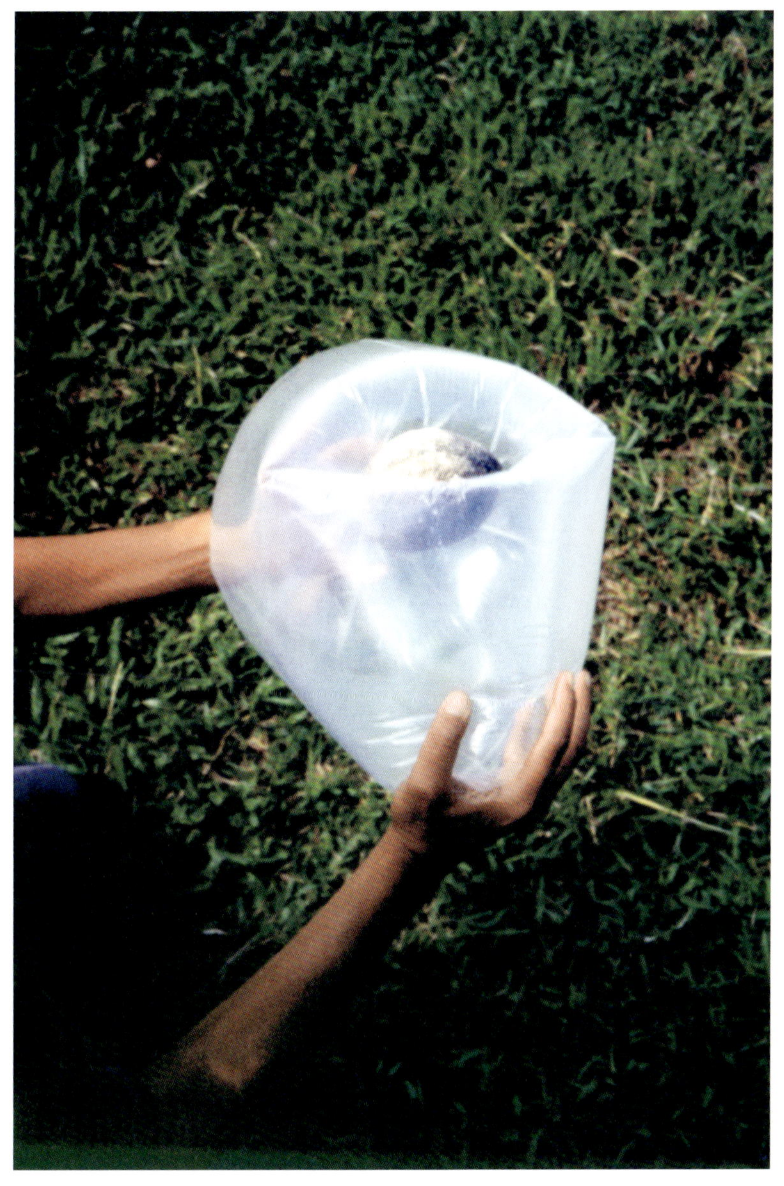

Lygia Clark, *Respire Comigo* (Breathe with me), 1966
rubber pipe, dimensions variable, photography by Sergio Zalis, 1983
courtesy Associação Cultural O Mundo de Lygia Clark

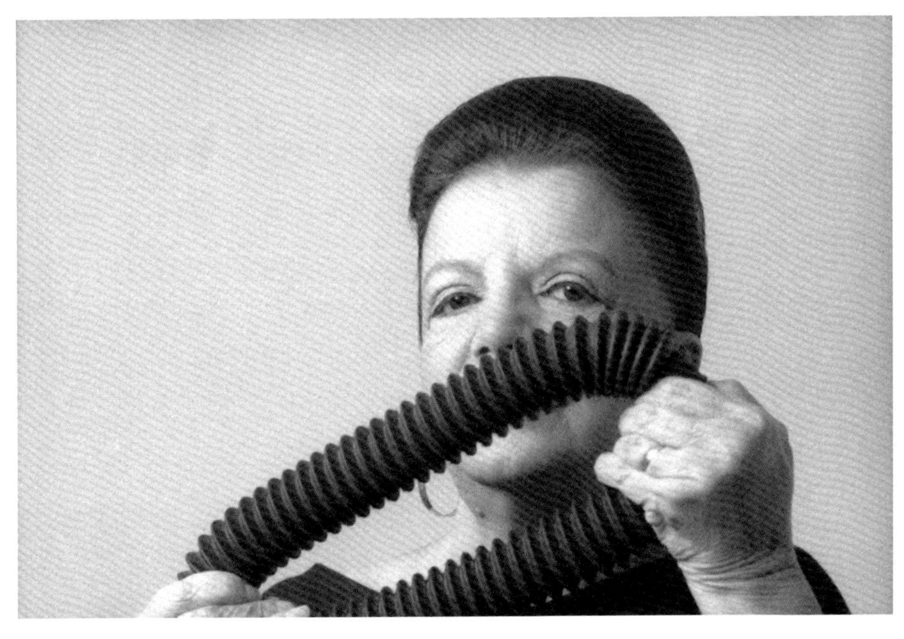

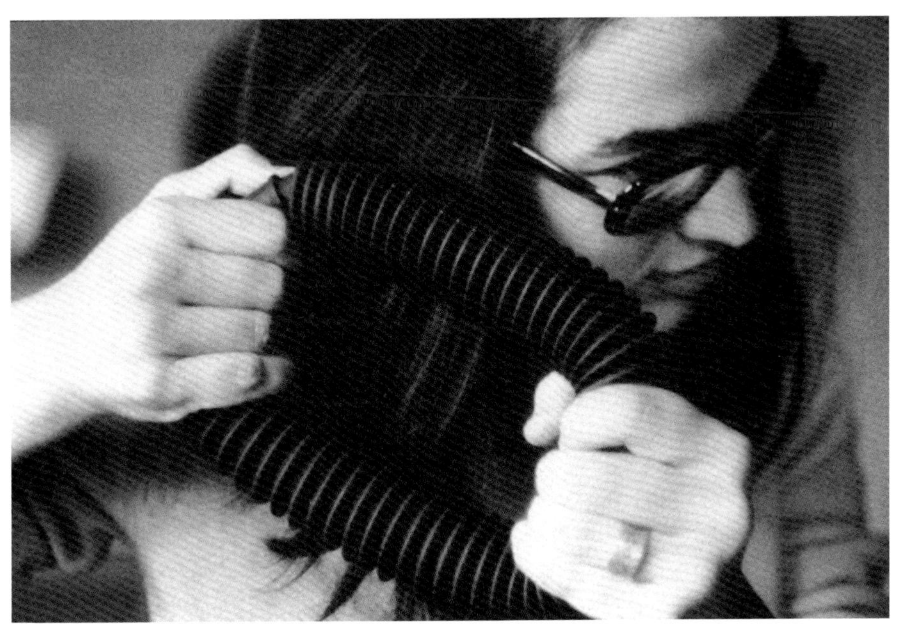

Lygia Clark, *O Eu e o Tu* (The I and the You), 1967
courtesy Associação Cultural O Mundo de Lygia Clark

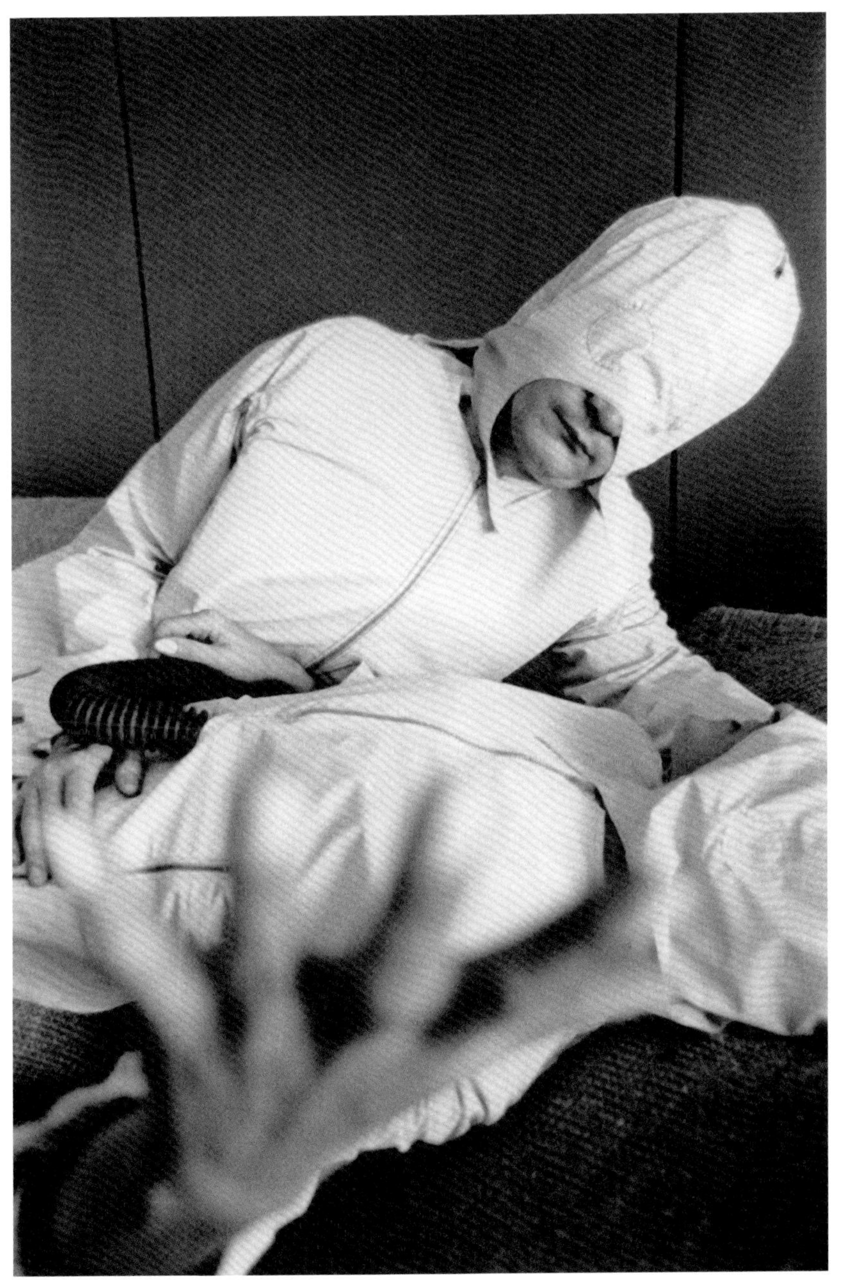

Lygia Clark, *Estruturas vivas – Mandala* (Live structures-Mandala), 1969
photograph by Hagége A, Paris, 1970, courtesy Associação Cultural O Mundo de Lygia Clark

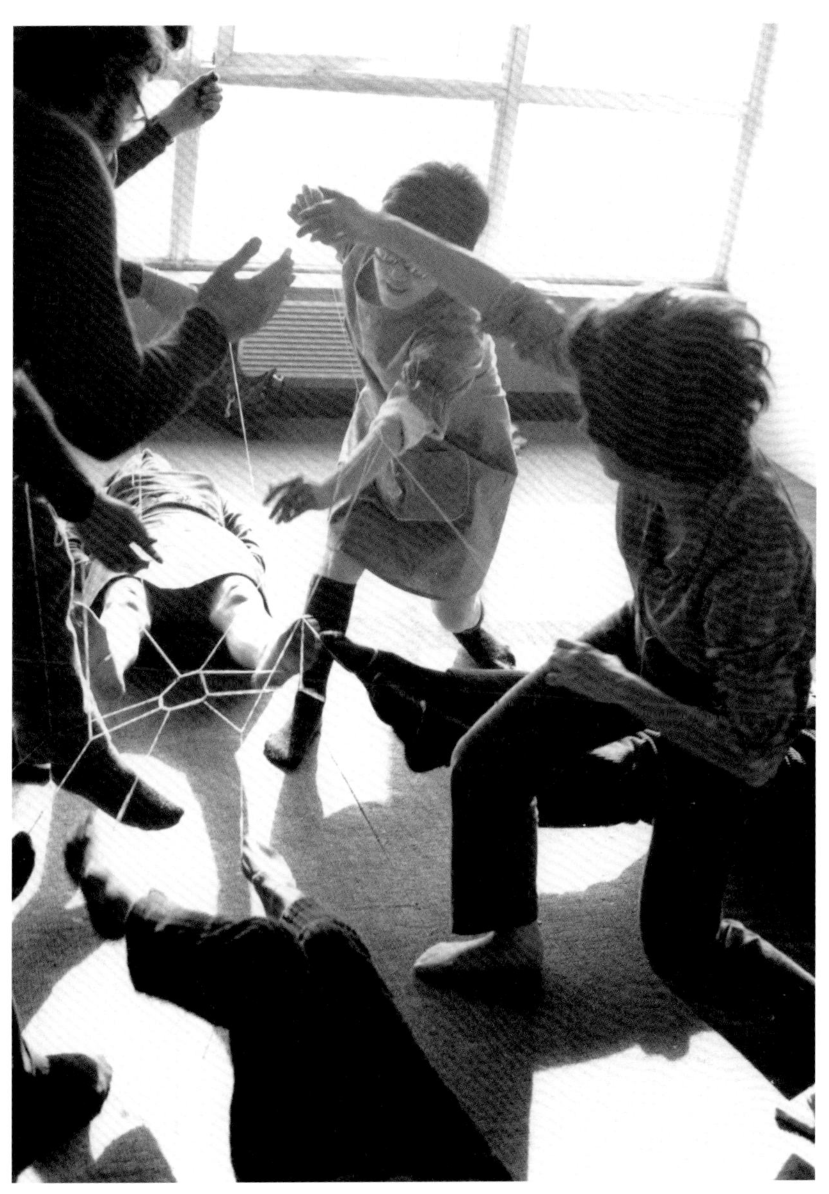

Sonia Boyce, *Portrait of Sonia Boyce*, 1995 →
installing PEEP exhibition, Royal Pavilion and Brighton Museum, UK
image courtesy InIVA – the Institute of International Visual Arts

Lygia Clark

Sonia Boyce

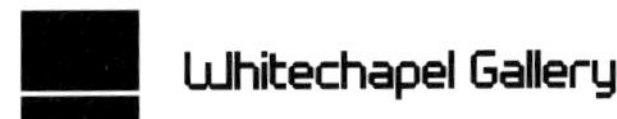
Whitechapel Gallery

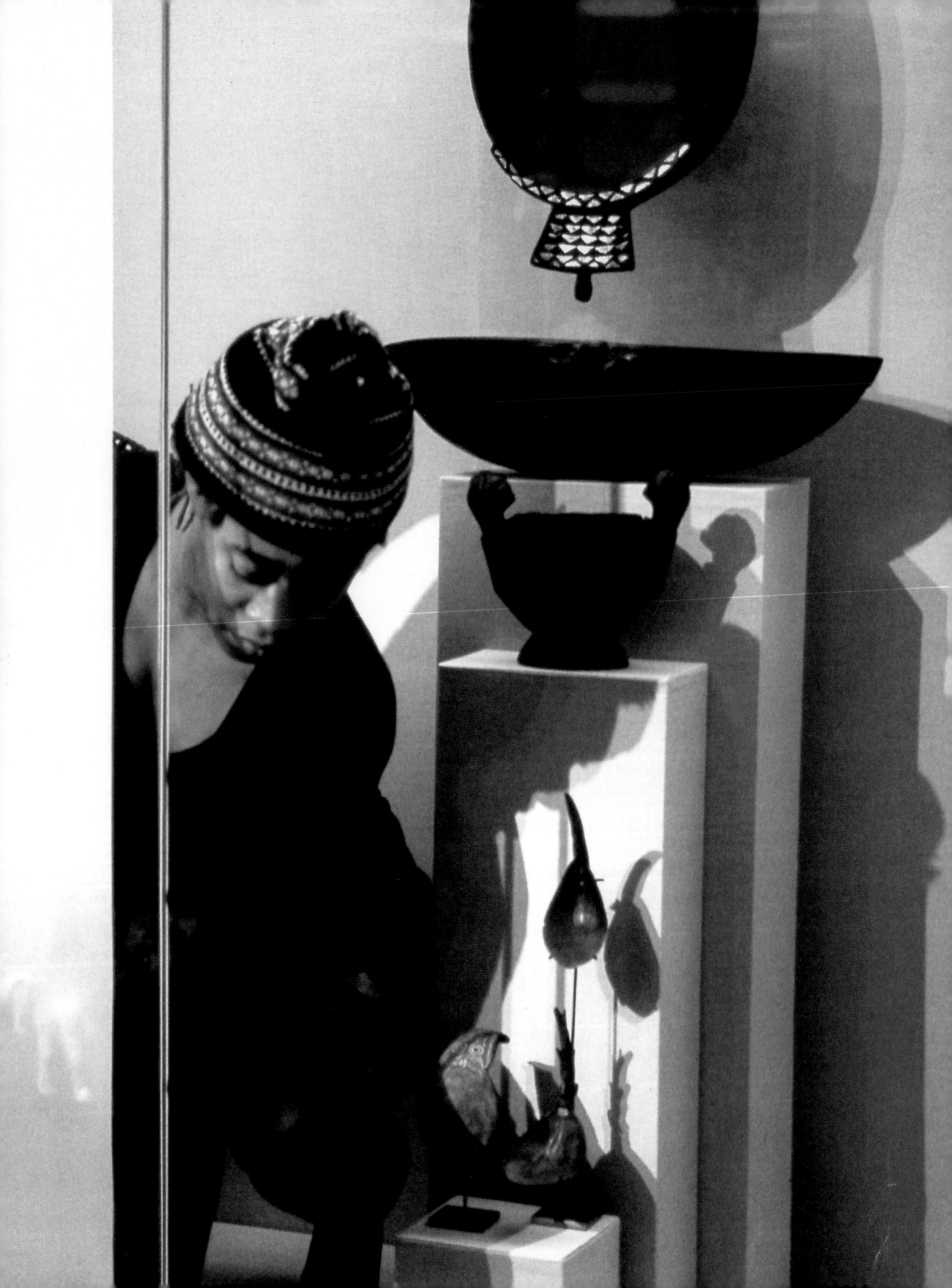